Rescue Matters

C.J. ENGLISH

To the millions of dogs that have suffered

when there were not enough resources for help,

you are not forgotten.

In order to maintain anonymity, in some instances places, names of individuals, identifying characteristics, and other recognizable factors have been changed. The following story is based on true events and told from my unique perspective and recollection. I recognize that individuals involved may have memories that are not the same as my own. There are also people and events not mentioned here that contributed to the success of the rescue.

Where identified, written material has been reprinted from its original author with permission. In order to maintain the authenticity of those stories, only minor grammatical changes have been made to provide clarity for the reader.

My conversations with Keith Benning happened over several years in person, over the phone, and through written correspondence. At times I've presented information from multiple conversations as a single conversation.

The opinions expressed in *Rescue Matters* are my own and do not necessarily reflect the opinion of Turtle Mountain Animal Rescue, Keith Benning, any other organization or individual mentioned in this book. In writing this book I mean no harm to anyone. It is my hope that by raising awareness about many of the issues presented, we can continue to come together and find solutions.

www.cjenglishauthor.com

Cover Design: Courtesy of Amanda Mckinnon at MSPIRE
www.mspire.com

Cover Photo: Glory. Courtesy of Amber Engebretson

Back Cover Photo: Keith Benning. Courtesy of Keith Benning

Editor: Nicole Hartney at Letter-Eye Editing

Paperback ISBN-13: 978-0-9863042-4-8

The digital version of *Rescue Matters* contains a full color photo gallery not available in print. Also included are live links that go directly to the original video footage of some of the events recounted here.

For an interactive experience consider downloading a copy to your e-reader. A generous portion of the profits from the sale of any version of this book will go directly back to Turtle Mountain Animal Rescue.

CONTENTS

FOREWORD		8
CHAPTER ONE	The Die Off	13
	Gypsy's Story	18
CHAPTER TWO	A Rescue is Born	21
CHAPTER THREE	The Outsider	31
CHAPTER FOUR	Hell On Earth	35
	Bear's Story	39
CHAPTER FIVE	Invisible Dogs	43
	Bubba's Story	48
CHAPTER SIX	The Deputy's Dogs	57
	Chance's Story	64
CHAPTER SEVEN	An Angel Is Born	65
	Smokey's Story	70
CHAPTER EIGHT	Angels Get Wings	73
	Lucas's Story	82
CHAPTER NINE		
Dogs Because People Suck		89
	John Doe Dog	94
CHAPTER TEN	A Cold Surrender	95
	Band of Brothers	101
CHAPTER ELEVEN	The Rescue Writer	105
	Fozzy's Story	112
CHAPTER TWELVE	Angels Fly	115
CHAPTER THIRTEEN	Shots Fired	129
CHAPTER FOURTEEN	Officer Down	135
	Pickle's Story	144
	Georgie's Story	146
CHAPTER FIFTEEN	300 Dead Dogs	149
	Arya's Story	158
CHAPTER SIXTEEN	Saving Bambi	161
CHAPTER SEVENTEEN		
Tragedy Rocks a Nation		167
	Daisy's Story	172
CHAPTER EIGHTEEN	Madeline	177
	Remington's Story	182
CHAPTER NINTEEN		
Turtle Mountain, Meet Harvey		185

CHAPTER TWENTY
  Turtle Mountain, Meet Irma 193
    Lenny's Story 197
CHAPTER TWENTY-ONE
  Now That's Just Bull Pit 203
    Brenda's Story 210
CHAPTER TWENTY-TWO
  TMAR Gets an Employee 215
CHAPTER TWENTY-THREE
    Eric & Rowdy 227
    Bella's Story 231
CHAPTER TWENTY-FOUR
  The Business of Saving Animals 237
    Losing Bubba 242
CHAPTER TWENTY-FIVE
    No-Kill TMAR 245
    Big Chief's Story 247
CHAPTER TWENTY SIX
    A New Code 249
    Hudson's Story 252
CHAPTER TWENTY-SEVEN
    ND, Your're Next 255
    Hope's Story 261
CHAPTER TWENTY-EIGHT
  Determined Rescue... 265
    Glory's Story 268
BONUS CHAPTER
  Handsome Rob's Story 275
AUTHOR'S NOTE 278
NEVER FORGOTTEN 280-283
ACKNOWLEDGMENTS 288
PHOTO CREDITS 288

FOREWORD

I first met Charmaine in the fall of 2015 when I was writing a story about her for *Fargo Monthly*. I knew immediately that she would be much more to me than just a subject I was writing about. We shared similar life experiences, we both love wine probably a little bit too much, we swear like sailors and we're both incredibly passionate and vocal about the things we care about.

While I was the editor for the magazine, I consistently reached out to Charmaine for her insight and had her write semi-monthly columns focused around health and well-being. One day in particular she asked me to meet with her about an idea that she had. I expected her to tell me about a new book project she was working on or maybe an idea for an upcoming article, but what we were about to talk about was something much bigger.

I spent two hours listening to Charmaine tell me about Turtle Mountain Animal Rescue, and how she had just taken part in a surrender event. My heart immediately sunk as she told me about the die-off and the number of dogs found frozen in the Turtle Mountain region. To this day, I still remember every detail about that coffee date and how it made me feel. I left feeling extremely heavy hearted, but also very much curious about what I could do to help. Do we fundraise using the connections we both had? Do I help her tell TMAR's story? We talked about a number of possibilities.

I spent the next year and a half as the editor of *Fargo Monthly* magazine advocating for the first ever pet issue, and by July

2016 I was finally able to pull it off with great public feedback. I made a point to focus on adoption, fostering and the importance of proper animal care. Charmaine was a contributor to that issue, and I'm glad I was able to give her another medium to share TMAR's story. That issue and her story opened my eyes even more to the importance of adoption and fostering, and how grave of a problem animal abuse, overpopulation and abandonment still are.

I can't think of a better person to tell this story. Charmaine is full of passion, grit, honesty and drive that many people lack when it comes to wanting change. In this book, there's a quote of hers that stood out to me, "I'm all for thoughts and prayers, but I'm more for policy and change." Truer words could never be spoken. I'm a firm believer that actions speak louder than words, and in this situation, we all need to be as loud and active as possible to keep seeing change.

Erica Rapp

We will be known forever by the tracks we leave.

- Dakota Sioux Proverb

When Keith Benning moved to Rolette County, North Dakota in the fall of 2013, he had no idea there was an animal overpopulation problem.

CHAPTER ONE

The Die Off

 Snow crunched under his heavy boots as Keith Benning walked toward the abandoned trailer. With each breath, a plume of white fog hit the air. The coldest, darkest days of winter had arrived. The die off had begun.

It was January in North Dakota on a remote square of land, a stone's throw from the Canadian border. If the forecast was true, the area was about to plunge into the deep freeze. Wind chills of thirty to fifty below zero were expected for another week, maybe longer.

With the deadly cold bearing down, every minute that passed was now life or death. If Keith didn't find them soon, they might not make it another night. Just before dark, he reccived a message.

There's a litter of puppies under an abandoned trailer. I threw food out, but I'm worried they're going to freeze. I haven't seen them in a few days. Can you help?

That message and an address was all Keith was told about the situation. Only he knew something else. If he didn't go, who would? In a conversation with Keith, he recalled what someone said to him just a few months earlier.

*A guy at work told me to stop, now. That people had tried to rescue animals in the past but everyone gave it up after six months. They all burned out. I remember telling him we were going to build an animal shelter. He laughed and told me, "I give it a year."

Whoever said that didn't know Keith. Looking away was not an option. He would prove not only to be fit for the job of rescuing animals, but would get the job done in a place no one else had succeeded before.

I asked him about the first dog he remembered taking into his home. That was when he told me about Grace, a stray that had been living on the streets and eating garbage to survive. Someone messaged Keith about a group of kids who were throwing rocks at her. Here, animal overpopulation is a problem so longstanding that to some, hungry dogs eating out of the dumpsters have become wallflowers, a thing to shoo away. To Keith and his wife** they were not invisible. They were animals suffering, and when someone or something is suffering, you help.

They took Grace in, cared for her, and eventually found her a permanent home. Keith didn't know it at the time, but she was the start of a new way of life for him. He had no intention of becoming the Dog Rescue Guy. He never imagined that four thousand animals would go through his hands over the next four years.

I followed my then wife up here for a job. At first it was like, *what the hell did I get myself into?* I walked into my house one night after work and found a pit bull standing on the kitchen counter eating out of a flour bag. You couldn't contain them all. Any area that could have a dog, did, and then some. We used sheets of plywood to separate the rooms. We'd have to move one board of plywood to get to the next area, then the next and the next. In the beginning, with a one bedroom house and no garage, dogs were in the living room, kitchen, hallway, basement, bathroom, anywhere and everywhere. I rigged up doggy gates and wood boards to separate them the best I could. Oh, and the house was all carpet too.

They kept every rescued animal safe until they could find it a home. After just a few months, the amount of work and responsibility became immense. They were housing nearly a dozen dogs at any one time. It was clear why no one had kept at it before. The problem was far greater than Keith realized or could manage. Calls and messages came in at all hours of the day and night. On the night he received the message about the puppies under the trailer, he was already overwhelmed with human calamities. There was nothing he could do for the puppies until after his shift. He hoped they would still be alive.

I had been at work since six in the morning. Domestic, child sexual assault, vehicle pursuit, stolen property, everyone wanted to be a jerk on that Thursday. I was supposed to be off at 6 p.m. but I was still at work at eight. I took the message and told the lady I would try and get over there. There was a girl in Bottineau that had offered to help with the rescue the week before so I reached out. She had never rescued before. I didn't have a choice so I connected the two and hoped for the best. Around eight-thirty [the volunteer] called and said she couldn't get to all the puppies but could see that two were dead, frozen. She was upset, confused, and scared. This wasn't supposed to be what rescue is like. Rescue was supposed to be like the commercial where you save the cold dog and squeeze it in your arms. This scene was just utter despair.

Home from work, Keith changed his clothes and rushed out to help. When he pulled up the trailer was not a residence, but a dilapidated shack that had long been abandoned. It was held up by crumbling cinder blocks and four feet of packed snow. A collapse seemed imminent.

There was no way under the trailer except a small opening where the momma dog had been crawling in and out. The snow was packed so tight I went around to the other side and found the smallest drift and started to dig. I wished I had brought gloves or a shovel, but you always think of that later. I dug and dug until I could get under the trailer.

First one dead puppy, then another then another. Momma was curled up in the middle of the trailer with one puppy near her. I hoped it was alive, but I couldn't get to it. The ground was frozen three feet deep and no matter how much I clawed at the dirt, I couldn't get under the cross beam of the trailer. I pulled out my knife and stabbed at the ground, but the blade didn't break past the first inch. As I backed out I saw how unstable the whole thing was. I went to the other side and dug again. I clawed and shanked the ground until I was able to exhale everything in my lungs and make it under. All dead.

Six puppies, about four months old, all ribs, a short life of being cold and hungry. Mom was huddled up in the dirt, defeated that she hadn't saved them.

I hooked a leash on her but she didn't want to go. She wanted to stay with her babies. I had to drag her out a foot at a time. My shirt and flannel rode up as I backed out and I could feel a pile of dried dirt rubbing on my stomach. I pulled and she pulled back until I felt the snow on my skin which meant we were almost out.

So where do you take a stray who is near death and has just lost all six of her puppies when there is no shelter, no humane society, no animal control and no help?

Home.

You take her home.

---

*As denoted by different formatting here and throughout the book, these select passages are Keith's writing. Minor punctuation and grammatical changes have been made but have not altered the original message.

**When Keith contacted his ex-wife about including her contributions into this story, she respectfully requested to not be part of this project. She is the co-founder of Turtle Mountain Animal Rescue (TMAR) and pivotal in its success early on. She was involved with countless rescue efforts and deserves to be credited with saving thousands of lives alongside Keith out of their home. Her tremendous sacrifice and heroism are not outlined in this story at her request, but what she has done has not been forgotten or discarded. There have been many instances throughout this story where "he" was actually "they," but in no way does not including her presence diminish or falsify the rescue efforts of Keith Benning himself.

Gypsy's Story

Rolette County, North Dakota – Shirley Morin

 "On my way home from work on Wednesday evening I saw a white box sitting in water in the ditch. I slowed down and saw a puppy poke her head out of the box. I stopped my car, got out and started calling to her. She crouched back inside the box. I don't know how long she was sitting in water, but her little paws were pinkish red. I drove up to my house, got my husband and called my brother to come help. We drove back down to the crossing and the puppy was still there. We both tried to call her and persuade her to come but she kept ducking back deeper in the box in the water. When my brother got there he went down the steep ditch, got her out of the water and brought her up to us. I took her right away and was reassuring her everything was going to be okay. She was shaking and cold and scared. Every time I went to touch her she flinched. I noticed how skinny she was. Her back bones were showing and her little hip bones were showing. Her paws were freezing cold. I sure hope whoever gets her knows how sweet she is and how much love she needs. Give her big hugs and tell her Momma said, 'Don't worry, everything will be okay'. Tell her how she is loved."

Shirley and her family brought Gypsy into their home, fed her and kept her warm and safe. They contacted Keith to see if he could help. With independent rescuers on the front lines and TMAR as a resource, Gypsy was moved through the rescue chain and eventually adopted.

CHAPTER TWO

A Rescue is Born

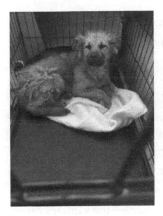 Keith's efforts to clean up the stray animal problem were immediately recognized and an entire county of people began looking to him for help. Within a year of moving to Rolette County, North Dakota, Keith turned his entire life and home into a makeshift animal shelter. Whether he intended to or not, and even if he didn't want it, it was done. A rescue was born.

The amount of phone calls and private messages he received from people asking for help was overwhelming. People wanted to see change and were willing to participate in solving the problem when help became available. Requests for support covered a gamut of issues that in any other city would be doled out among several entities like volunteer organizations, low cost or free vet services, and municipal divisions. Here, there was just Keith.

My dog had a litter of puppies and we can't keep them we already have six dogs, can you help?

There's a dog in our backyard with a broken leg. When can you be here?

My aunt died and we can't take her dogs, can you come and take them? I don't want to call the dogcatcher.

There's a dog outside our school that looks really skinny. We don't know what to do with him. Can you pick him up? Quick?

At any one time, hundreds of stray and unwanted dogs roamed in a county that occupies roughly 1 percent of the state, a county that has no affordable or accessible resources to solve the problem. Until Keith, the only solution was the dogcatcher, and if he was your fate . . . your fate was sealed.

For the families that wanted to help stray and starving animals, but didn't see it fit to call the dogcatcher, their only option was to take the animals in themselves, or find them a new home. That is what many families here have done for decades. They are the independent rescuers—the families on the front lines, operating in the shadows out of their homes and garages, taking in one or one hundred animals. These folks ask for no credit and get no glory, but they save lives every day, year after year, decade after decade.

These independent rescuers are the good stewards within struggling communities who play a pivotal role in shaping local attitudes toward strays, encouraging responsible pet ownership and advocating for the humane treatment of animals. They are the individuals who don't look away when they see a dog eating garbage out of a dumpster, they find a way to help her.

. . .

I live in Fargo, North Dakota, about four hours from Keith. If there are stray animals, there is not only help, but choices—multiple entities with the sole purpose of helping humans or animals in need. I can call animal control, the Humane Society, or one of the many smaller rescue organizations.

It wasn't until I began to help in animal rescue that I realized how important and necessary these often volunteer-based organizations are. They save lives, alleviate suffering and reunite humans with their lost companions. It wasn't until I began to help in animal rescue that I realized the good fortune and privilege animals born into my 58104 zip code have. For that, I am eternally grateful and will never forget that with great privilege comes a greater responsibility.

Things are different north of where I live. Not all zip codes in North Dakota, or any state for that matter, have good systems for animal control, such as a Humane Society, or SPCA (Society for the Prevention of Cruelty to Animals.) But in one North Dakota county, an unlikely hero and new resource had sprung.

Word spread that the new deputy not only took in animals, but was successful at finding them homes. Keith's newly-appointed status as the Dog Rescue Guy expanded into tasks an entire rescue organization takes on with a team of volunteers and adequate funding to support it.

Keith became the CEO, the secretary, the staff and the cleaning crew of a growing operation. He was also thrust into the role of judge, jury and executioner; having to make unthinkable decisions no human should have to make, the kind of decisions that cut deep and leave scars.

It was a great thing that a majority of the community wanted to help. It was bad that what was being asked of the newly-appointed rescue guy would come with tremendous strains on his time, checkbook, sanity and relationships. Yet, when you have compassion and heart mixed with grit like Keith, instead of quitting, you dig in.

Keith worked full time as a deputy. After all day shifts, he rescued animals around the clock. His life plunged into a groundhog-day cycle of eating, sleeping and breathing rescue work. He slogged through day-after-day answering calls, responding to messages, picking up dogs, cats, puppies and kittens. He coordinated transport or drove them himself, hauling dozens of animals thousands of miles to no-kill shelters where they would eventually be adopted. His entire existence became consumed by all things rescue.

He worked with other rescues to take in the dogs he picked up and made endless road trips to the vet for supplies. He had to learn how to bottle-feed orphaned pups, find time to pick hundreds of ticks out of matted fur and pull quills from scared, hungry dogs. He would somehow have to sleep while puppies howled, barked and cried each night. Keith was up at dawn every morning to feed, water and clean kennels before his shift at the station began again. Dizzying and exhausting doesn't come close to describing the madness and burnout that came with having a garage rescue. Armies have accomplished less.

We brought one pregnant dog after another to the vet. Each one more emaciated than the last. The vet didn't know how they were even still alive. They came in with everything from mange to parvo. All of them starving. Some had broken backs, legs and gunshot wounds.

Ninety-mile trips to the closest vet were tiresome, emotionally draining, and often traumatizing. Not to mention bank breaking. Within months of taking in stray animals, Keith had amassed thousands of dollars in debt from vet bills and associated costs of sheltering a dozen animals at any one time. Still, like a shipwreck victim clinging to the lifeboat, he was determined not to let go and drown. Even under the most insurmountable circumstances, he found the strength to keep going and stay optimistic about making a difference. He was past the point of no return. Keith had to figure out how to become a sustainable garage rescue without burning out. He started a Facebook page and a GoFundMe campaign to ask for help with vet bills. Even though it was a long shot, he hoped that one day, he could raise enough money to build a real shelter.

The first step was to ask the community for help by recruiting volunteers from the area. There was already a network of independent rescuers out there doing the work. He would just need to find them so they could put their heads and efforts together. On the lookout for independent rescuers, Keith met an ambitious college student who was known for taking in strays. Lacey Strietzel is a mom with a big heart and a gentle way about her. She'd grown up there and had been taking dogs into her home steadily for more than a year. She too was experiencing the same kind of burnout and overwhelming sense of burden rescue work can bring.

Keith, his wife, and Lacey teamed up and founded Turtle Mountain Animal Rescue (TMAR.) They were no longer just random people taking in dogs. They were an organization; a legitimate nonprofit with a vision to save lives and alleviate suffering. They had a name, a mission, and Keith was leading the charge as the most public figure among them working to gain trust within the community.

During my many conversations with Keith about those early days when TMAR was founded, he kept going back to how pivotal his wife and Lacey were in the beginning, how he couldn't have done it without their help. I asked Lacey, who has since stepped away from rescue work to pursue a career in nursing and raise her family, to tell me about those early days when the rescue was just formed.

"I did help them occasionally," she said. "It was only when we had surrender events or picking up a dog to bring to his house when I was free from school. Keith has put so much into this rescue, which is why I feel that Keith and his wife should get the full credit." She went on to say that Keith deserves to be appreciated for his hard work and big heart.

Within TMAR today, no one person wants, asks or needs credit for the volunteer work they do. In fact, if you ask anyone involved, each person gives credit to the next person, or to the whole team. This is one of the reasons TMAR has been so successful in its efforts; the core volunteers function as a cohesive team. There is no one rogue cowboy, no authoritarian or string puller, not even Keith. He's a humble, hard-working, never-give-up kind of guy who wants no credit. This book, because it highlights his many extraordinary merits and fearless skills, has made him squirm more than once.

Keith deserves more credit than he probably has the capacity to accept. Which is why I was shocked when I learned that not everyone trusted his intentions—and even more stunned when I found out that his efforts were met with suspicion, gossip, envy and sabotage.

...

Just months after its conception, the fledgling rescue was nearly torn apart by local politics, rumors, lies and sabotaged by naysayers. TMAR and Keith were swept under the rug by state and tribal officials. But the spirit of one man wasn't so easily broken. Something bigger, more powerful than all of the obstacles that lay ahead had been set in motion.

A revolution had begun.

One that would prove to be unstoppable.

1.2.3.4.5.6.7.8.9.10.11.12.13.14.15.16.17.18.1
9.20.21.22.23.24.25.26.27.28.29.30.31.32.33.3
4.35.36.37.38.39.40.41.42.43.44.45.46.47.48.4
9.50.51.52.53.54.55.56.57.58.59.60.61.62.63.6
4.65.66.67.68.69.70.71.72.73.74.74.76.77.78.7
9.80.81.82.83.84.85.86.87.88.89.90.91.92.93.9
4.95.96.97.98.99.100..
....
....
....
....
....
....

...........163.

CHAPTER THREE

The Outsider

The reservation was a different world that you have to live and work on to understand. I was an outsider, a white guy on the rez trying to change things, so everyone looked for a deeper motive but there wasn't one. I had to learn a lot of things the hard way. If I am going to be a guest on someone else's land, I needed to understand and respect them and their culture. I learned about the importance of family, ceremony, pride, and traditions.

I asked Keith about his vision to raise money for the rescue in the beginning. "Donation boxes," he said with a chuckle. I laughed too, imagining a cardboard cutout with a picture of a sad dog and a slot barely big enough for a quarter. Quarters would help, but it was dollars that were needed to solve the problem.

It never occurred to me to reach out for help beyond the local community.

To really make an impact and decrease the number of stray and unwanted animals, a long-term sustainable solution was needed. That solution would require enough money for transport vehicles, staff and community outreach programs. Free or low-cost vaccination clinics, spay and neuter clinics in addition to raising enough money to buy land for a shelter would also be necessary. Money would need to be raised to take care of the ongoing building, business and animal care expenses a shelter would require. This was no job for petty change, and without most of those divisions in place and functioning well, a solution would never become a reality.

Asking a community to give money that's already scarce was a doomed vision before it was conceived. This community needed help from the outside-in to be able to make changes from the inside-out. Keith was the only person in a position to build a bridge that needed to be crossed both ways. But trying to make changes in a place where trust is earned, not given, requires exceptional patience.

> When we started the rescue many people were against us and thought there was some kind of scam behind it. They thought someone else was coming in to screw over the reservation in some way. I can't blame them, that's what has happened over and over. I did what I could to defend myself and what I was doing (rescuing dogs). I wanted to make sure everyone knew I wasn't out to screw anyone, or get rich off of the problem. I just wanted to save dogs and be a good cop.

Local support for the surprise rescue was a hard sell. Relations became increasingly turbulent when the rescue was repeatedly accused of "stealing dogs and selling them for profit," as purported through rumors and lies. It was a falsehood that unfortunately spread like a virus even without proof of such allegations. Any progress Keith made in gaining trust from the community took two steps back when a new accusation spread. TMAR "stealing dogs" is a disillusioned lie that still lingers in the distance today and undermines ongoing rescue efforts. Luckily, that unfounded notion remains dormant most of the time, but once in a while, someone coughs it up and spreads it again.

There are so many stray and unwanted animals everywhere in the world. To anyone involved in animal rescue, stealing dogs is preposterous. Everyone who got to know Keith came to understand how untrue those rumors were, and how much he was personally sacrificing to save animals. It was also understandable why some of the locals felt that way. There did seem to be a lot of disappearing companion animals for such a small area. Nearly every week Keith posted to the TMAR Facebook page about a missing dog to help spread the word and hopefully reunite them.

The community would eventually come around and fall in love with Keith, as would the whole nation, through his real-life rescues. First he would have to become the liaison between two worlds that have a history of colliding and distrusting each other since the beginning of time.

> Many Native people are suspicious of outsiders, especially white people. If I gave someone an acknowledgment—a nod, smile, hello—I almost always got it back. But that was just scratching the surface. Being polite and gaining someone's respect are two totally different things.

Most of the areas in the county where Keith served as the Dog Rescue Guy, were predominately Native American. He would have to learn their language (literally and figuratively) and gain trust on all sides of the invisible boundaries between state and tribal land. He would need to build a bridge where a bridge had never been built before. That would take breaking down stereotypes held strong for decades, and it would take the changing of hearts and minds filled with preconceived notions that have kept everyone at arm's length.

To stop the cycle of birth and die off here, Keith would have to convince the local tribe that he was a suitable spokesperson who could advocate on behalf of the animals without taking advantage of the people. On the other side of the line, Keith would have to somehow remind people that what was going on was not a reservation problem, but a humanitarian one.

Outsiders and insiders, borders and cultures, divisions and classes, none of that mattered—animals were dying. Animal welfare mattered.

Whose fault it was that a problem existed or who was responsible for cleaning it up was clear—humans. No more fingers needed to be pointed.

Perhaps fate does know what she's doing when she moved Keith up to God's country. Slowly he gained their trust, one person at a time, by serving the very community that didn't trust him. As it turns out, Keith had a bit of a checkered past with a unique skill set, making him perfectly suited for the job of bridge builder, negotiator and diplomat.

CHAPTER FOUR

Hell on Earth

Sixty acres of despair surrounded by 33-foot concrete walls lined with gun towers is how Keith described the maximum-security prison. I asked him how he felt on the last day he walked out of the notorious place dubbed by some of the inmates as "Hell on Earth."

> I was literally thinking WOW, I can't believe I made it out alive.

A Google search of Stateville Correctional Facility in Crest Hill, Illinois, turns up images and statistics that blow my mind. My afternoon writing quickly turned into falling down a rabbit hole of articles and videos about life inside an underworld I couldn't begin to fathom. Among other things, Stateville is known for executing John Wayne Gacy, the Killer Clown. The barbarian responsible for single-handedly turning a beloved comedy character into a terrifying monster that inspired Steven King to write the book *It*.

After a few YouTube videos of what life is like on the inside of Stateville, I picked my tongue up off the floor, pushed my eyeballs back into their sockets, picked up my phone and sent him a text.

Holy shit! I can't believe you survived Stateville. Call me!

Keith didn't respond right away. He was en route to pick up three puppies that had just been born under a structure on someone's property. When I finally connected with him I could hear tires on the pavement, a common sound when I'm talking to Keith on the phone. Also in the background of our conversation was the dinging of an alarm warning system reminding him to put his seat belt on—a dinging that never seems to quit.

We chatted about rescue business, where the puppy pick-up was, their condition, and what would be their fate. Then I let him know I'd just been thoroughly entangled by the Internet for hours, reading about his ex employer. We exchanged expletives and shared a laugh at the extreme circumstances from which he'd survived.

Keith worked at Stateville for six of a fifteen-year stint as a prison guard. As we talked more in depth about his experience, I was impressed by my interesting and incorruptible friend. I realized he has lived his entire life honing the skills required to win over the hearts and minds of even the most hardened criminals.

> Everything in prison comes down to respect. If you show a convict respect they'll show it back. What keeps you from getting killed is respect.

He told me about several instances when he was being surrounded by men with bad intentions. He was outnumbered in each occurrence. But because not a day went by that he didn't treat every inmate with dignity, the imminent attack was called off by someone at the top of the intricate inmate hierarchy. On many occasions the inmates saved Keith from the same kind of trauma he saved them from every day. It was clear that he took his job seriously. He was a fair and open-minded guard who protected them from each other, and protected the outside world from them.

The former prison guard schooled me about a world of corruption and gangs, mental illness and tragedy, saviors and monsters. As he talked, I became more aware than ever that Keith had the skills, determination, and just enough crazy to do what no one else had done.

> I would literally say to myself each day before I went in, don't die today. Don't get raped today. We all had to look out for each other and just try to survive.

But not everyone did survive. There were many guards who lost their lives within those prison walls. The exact number is difficult to discern. Much of what happens there seems to be shrouded behind a political veil with stipulations like if they were attacked but died later in a hospital, it doesn't count.

As I talked with Keith I learned about the buckshots that peppered the ceiling in the now closed roundhouse, the suicides, stabbings and deaths of fellow officers. I was saddened by the cruel conditions for everyone under the roof at Stateville. I asked him how accurate the documentaries I'd been sucked into watching were. He was quite adamant that what the film crew saw was all a setup, a fake. Apparently, what I'd watched on the documentaries was a total joke and misrepresentation of what it was actually like inside.

It NEVER looked like that. They never showed the shit and piss and blood and chaos that was reality. Administrators made everything look great. We had guns with bent barrels, had to wade through water in places, and there were dirty guards who let inmates get stabbed in the showers. There were good ones, but there were bad ones too. It was so loud in there you had to scream to hear the person next to you. They literally barked like dogs. But the hardest thing about working in a prison is not getting sucked into the giant hole of negativity. No one wants to be there.

I was transfixed and could have stayed on the phone for hours as he told me about the reality of what life was like inside. Keith had story after story, each tale more unfathomable than the last. The man who lit himself on fire before hanging himself, riots, dodging balls of fire, milk cartons filled with sun-ripened urine and feces, pubic hair in his meals, drain cleaner in his drink, co-workers caught smuggling heroine in through their rectum, cockroaches everywhere and Sparky, the electric chair. At the end of our conversation I felt like I'd just watched the worst parts of *The Shawshank Redemption, The Green Mile* and *Locked Up Abroad*.

I understood at a deeper level who Keith was, the hell he'd come from and the skill it took to survive. The irony was not lost on me that my tall, broad-shouldered friend, a burly dude with an unmistakable air of authority survived six years inside Stateville without being assaulted, raped or killed, was now guarding the lives of . . . puppies. Surely, if he could survive serial killers he could handle a few puppies. Right?

Bear's Story

 Bear growled and showed his teeth when Keith approached. If he couldn't be handled, he would have to be put down. The city made the call that he was going to be shot in the morning if Keith wasn't able to take him. Off duty, Keith went to check out the situation.

Bear's owner had been arrested and was in prison where he wouldn't get out, ever. Bear was being cared for by a kind lady, but she could no longer handle him. The scars across his head and face were painful clues of what he'd been through, but Bear's life and circumstances up until that day were unknown.

When Keith approached, Bear let him know he wasn't going anywhere without a fight. "Screw this, I thought. I can't take that dog." Then in true Keith style, he tried again and again and again. No luck. Bear was too terrified or ferocious, or both to be handled. With great sadness Keith decided there was nothing he could do. He got back in his vehicle. He had no choice because sometimes, there is no choice.

From the outside looking in, it's easy to see a solution. *Turn Bear over to someone who can handle him. Don't put him down, just find a place that can rehabilitate him, train him, maybe he could be a police dog!*

These suggestions sound fantastic, but who is this miracle person and where are they located? There are no services anywhere near here for a thousand miles that can handle a case like Bear's. There is no animal training and rehabilitation facility sprawled out over dozens of acres with experienced handlers where Bear could be dropped off. Even if there was a place somewhere far away, where would he stay until he could go? Who would find that place? How would he get there? Who is going to be responsible for a dog that could kill you or your other pets until a home is found for him?

These are the complex questions without easy answers that animal rescuers must not only face but figure out. This would be only one of many times where Keith would be forced to make a decision that either saves or ends a life.

I could feel the pain in his voice when Keith told me about having to turn away from Bear. He has a special fondness for the regal German Shephard. Bear reminded him of Valkyrie, his own German Shephard and long-time companion who was waiting for him at home.

I just couldn't drive away. I told myself that I was going to try again. One more time.

Keith got out of his car and opened the back seat door as wide as it would go. He approached the scared dog, but this time Keith didn't back down.

Get in.

His voice was firm and he made a motion toward the open car door.

Bear jumped in. That was how I got Bear.

He bit me every time I touched him. If you tried to get him to go out or do something he would bite you if you grabbed his collar. Not hard enough to break the skin, but hard enough to let you know he wasn't going to be made to do anything. It was his defense mechanism. This great big ferocious dog was like a scared little kid. We fed him by hand for weeks until we could both finally handle him. It took two straight months of working with him every day to get him to where he was somewhat of a normal dog.

To this day, if he hears a gun or sees my gun, even if he hears the shell or bullet in the chamber he freaks out and tries to get out of the house. He's jumped through the living room window. When he hears a loud noise outside and wants to come back in he won't wait to go through the door, he'll jump through whatever window he can to get into the house. He'll rip right through the screen to get in. But he's still the best dog we've ever had—except for the whole window screen part. He protects the outside dogs against coyotes and has even chased off a mountain lion.

I never asked Keith why he kept Bear and didn't try to find a home for him after he was deemed a normal dog. Maybe he kept him because Hope needed Bear, like Bubba needed Bella or . . . and well, that's what happens in rescue. You end up with an annoying cat and a pile of dogs in your bed every night.

CHAPTER FIVE

Invisible Dogs

Rolette County is one of the most underserved counties in North Dakota. An isolated position on the map, brutal living conditions in the winter, along with high unemployment make it a challenging place to thrive.

From 2010 to 2017, unemployment in Rolette County bounced between 8% and 16%. The average unemployment rate for the state of North Dakota from 2008 to 2018 was just 2.5% to 4.5%.* making Rolette County's unemployment rate twice as high. That means there are so few jobs, that any one minimum wage opening has competition far greater than elsewhere in the state. So even if you want a job, there are very few to be found. Many residents stay with their roots and make their own way; there are families that are thriving. But others leave, and some, even if they want to leave and find a place with more opportunities, don't have the support they need to make it happen. People are suffering because there are so few jobs and where people are suffering, animals are suffering.

The state of North Dakota has a high school graduation rate of 85%. In Rolette County it's 65%. Relative to the state as a whole, the county reports performing poorly in the following areas: premature death, poor or fair physical and mental health, low birth weight, adult smoking, adult obesity, teen birth rates, child poverty, death from injuries, excessive drinking, lack of housing and insufficient numbers of primary care physicians and dentists.** The very definition of underserved just might be an understatement to the families that are trying to get by. Perhaps the invisible dogs that roam here are symbolic of a forgotten people.

Within Rolette County lie the Turtle Mountains. Now if you come from Montana, Wyoming or Alaska, these mountains are more like bunny hills, nevertheless, it's a forested, pristine landscape at least a little more above sea level than the rest of ND. This wooded haven is touted as Northern North Dakota and Southern Manitoba's best-kept secret. A trip along scenic Byway 43 will take you through small towns where people still exist with funny Northlandian accents and a niceness not found elsewhere in the world. In spite of the minus forty degree temperatures, the folks up here are as hardworking and hearty as they come.

Just beyond the county looking down at night from thirty-five thousand feet, the surrounding stateside is lit up with flares for a hundred miles across the Bakken formation. The estimated seven or more billion barrels of oil that is hidden deep underground here will likely produce an ebb and flow of traffic to the area for years, perhaps decades. As oil prices fluctuate there is either a feast or famine of jobs across many industries. The most recent boom that flooded the state with jobs and money has fizzled out, leaving much of western North Dakota reminiscent of a ghost town straight out of an old western movie.

The Turtle Mountain Tribe also resides within Rolette

County, existing as an autonomous government with sovereign status still today. The band of Chippewa Indians in these parts proudly refer to themselves as Anishinabe, (A-KNEE-Sheen-Ha-Bee) meaning the original people. With a rich and long Native American history, much of their culture is still woven into this area today. From the artwork in the community center to the traditions upheld and passed on in tight family circles, the Chippewa spirit is ever present. If you look closely, there are clues that much of the area and traditions exist in a time capsule—aspects of a way of life that have been preserved despite the quickly changing outside world.

The history of this land is as difficult as it is beautiful. In October of 2018, the *New York Times* reported that the Turtle Mountain Reservation had a 59 percent unemployment rate.*** There is a secret suffering here. Living among the last of the tall grass prairie, their howls have been forgotten in the shadow of human hardship. Though some are hiding in the brush, most are not actually invisible at all. They are the wallflowers that exist alongside a life that keeps going with or without them. These are the animals that, for decades, have slowly been forgotten and became invisible.

These invisible dogs are in every state across the nation, residing in areas where socio-economic struggles have yet to meet good solutions. Every city has pockets, every state guilty of whole areas overpopulated with domestic dogs and cats—without enough resources to reduce the numbers and ease suffering. Rolette County and the Turtle Mountain area are one of a handful of North Dakota's blind spots where the domestic dog and cat population has been left unmanaged not just for years, but decades.

The only system of check and balance here is the yearly die-off. Each year hundreds of dogs, puppies, cats and kittens freeze or starve to death in the unforgiving winter. When the snow melts and the rivers flood in the spring, those souls who survived begin the cycle again. They breed, puppies are born, and the endless circle of birth and death continues. Year after year, decade after decade. Not even nature with all her power and might can destroy enough of them to stop it. Each year she leaves just enough animals in the breeding population to keep this cruel loop in a never ending state of suffering.

I was talking to a friend of mine who'd recently been to Texas on an animal rescue trip. While she was there, someone said to her, "Your dogs are the lucky ones."

Baffled by the statement, I didn't understand why our dogs, the strays that freeze to death, were somehow the lucky ones. My heart was devastated by what came next.

"At least you have a die-off," the woman said. "The dogs here, [in Texas] suffer for years in the heat. They are starving and have mange that rips open their skin. They roam the streets for years before dying. At least some of yours are saved from years of suffering."

Heart.

Broken.

It was a reality that I knew already, but that didn't always hit me in the heart the way this fact check did. She was right. Ours are the lucky ones.

The volume of animals suffering in struggling communities across the world is staggering. Perhaps more than nature herself as an executioner can bear to take away. I am forced to think that domestic animal overpopulation is a problem too big for any one county, city or state to manage, or it wouldn't be a problem. I have to wonder if the problem TMAR was trying to solve needed something much smaller than a government with all its bureaucratic hoops and snail-like progress to get the job done. Perhaps the problem needed a fresh eye and dedicated heart—a man with unique skills and stickability. Someone who wouldn't give up—couldn't give up.

Giving up is not something Keith Benning knows how to do, making what came next unthinkable.

*Source: Labor Market Information Center, Job Service North Dakota, Local Area Unemployment Statistics
**2015 Community Health Assessment.
***   https://www.nytimes.com/2018/10/30/us/politics/north-dakota-voter-id.html

Bubba's Story

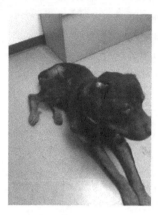

Keith had been working as a deputy sheriff for a year when he heard about Bubba. A former officer stopped Keith on the street and said he couldn't believe Bubba had survived as many winters as he had.

Bubba lived at the end of a ten-foot chain in a broken dog house surrounded by a yard filled with plywood and junk. Although he did get let in once in a while, Bubba was gravely malnourished and had a severe case of mange. More than half of his hair was gone, he had multiple skin infections, and once again, winter was coming.

Not long after I met Keith, I had the opportunity to meet Bubba. Like a proud dad would boast about his children, Keith told me all about Bubba. He warned me that Bubba was still in rough shape even though it had been a while since his rescue. He said that the years of being outside in the cold, at times starving, had eaten away at his body. Then he told me what it took to save him.

An older guy that used to be a cop stopped to talk to me. He brought up Bubba and said someone should take him away from his owner. He couldn't believe Bubba had made it through as many winters as he did alive. He told me about a time when it was forty below and the wind was howling. The only thing Bubba had to keep warm were some thin blankets inside of his house. The guy said that he stopped in front of the house and saw Bubba shivering.

"I never saw a living thing so cold in my life."

He called the police. They came out and told [the owner] that he needed to put some straw in the house or bring Bubba inside. The guy threw another blanket out but that was it. He called the police again a few hours later and Bubba's owners brought him inside for the night, but he was back out there the next day. I told him I would go over and take a look at Bubba.

Bubba lived across from a school next to a pile of plywood but he was always curled up in his dog house. When I started out there as a deputy I didn't know he was there even though I drove past the house ten times a day. When I got to the house, Bubba came out barking and growling. I noticed he was skinny and moved slowly due to arthritis. I was able to give him a dog treat but wasn't able to get close to his dog house. I thought about it, and in most states it would be neglect, but not North Dakota. I had been a deputy for a year at this point and had only won one neglect case. I knocked on the door but nobody answered. I called the state's attorney and told him the situation and sent him pictures. He said I would have to wait until it got colder, and Bubba got thinner, or had an injury or condition that needed vet care.

I drove by every day and felt like shit now that I knew he was there and needed help. I ran it all through my head. I knew he was hungry but if I fed him it would make the case harder. If I went to the door and talked to the people and told them they need to take care of him better, they might, but I knew he had to get away from them. If I did that, then what if it's winter and they throw him outside while I'm on my day off and he freezes and dies? So I drove past every day and tried to not look at the house or him. I let him suffer until he was suffering enough that I could win a case and get him out of there. I would think about him at home, at work, and every time I drove by. For awhile I tried to avoid that block. I would turn before it or do a loop around it and keep patrolling. Then I stopped seeing him for awhile. They started taking him inside more or I would just see the chain leading out to the pit that he had made in his dog house.

November rolled around and I started watching my weather app every day. What was the temp? What was the wind? Was it going to stay cold for a few days? Finally, in mid-November it got cold and windy with freezing rain and some snow. This was enough I thought. I walked into the yard and saw the black shape in the dog house. "Hey buddy, how ya doing?" He started to snarl and bark and try to charge out of his dog house. He made it out the door and fell over, struggling to get up. He looked like a zombie. Forty percent of his fur was gone and he was nothing but skin and bones. He stumbled forward and I held out a treat. He wolfed it down and looked for more. I had waited too long. Why in the hell did I do that? Why didn't I go up sooner?

His body condition and mange was so bad I was sure I could have stepped in much sooner and won a case. I felt like shit. I felt lower than shit. I was a horrible person for letting this happen. I went to my car and got him a full bowl of food and a gallon jug of water. One good meal and drink would do nothing to make his outward condition better, but I had to keep him going at this point. From the looks of him he only had a week or two left.

I took pictures of everything. I got in my car, drove off, and sent everything to the state's attorney. He said we had more than enough for a case, but we would have to get a judge to sign off on a warrant to seize him. I told him to call whatever judge he could because it was supposed to get cold and I didn't know if he would make it. Then I waited. Time was in slow motion that day, and every time I called to check there was still nothing. The state's attorney had emails out to every judge in the area, but one had lost a parent, another was out of town, and things had gone nowhere. Four o'clock rolled around and still nothing. It was a Friday and I was just mad. Mad at the state laws, mad at the owner, mostly mad at myself. Do I put a blanket down? Does that make them know something is up and lock him away in the house? Still nothing at four-thirty so I called again but the state's attorney was gone. His assistant said no word from the judges.

Sit and wait some more. Sit and let him suffer some more. Saturday and Sunday crawled. I did nothing. He had to make it two more days. He had to. I waited until dark and snuck up and gave him food and water. Monday came around and the judge issued a warrant. I flew to the house and saw he wasn't outside. Had he died? Was I too late? I called the state's attorney and asked if I could go to the door for the warrant. He read it again and said no. The warrant said it was for the dog on the chain outside of the house. Going to the door wouldn't work. Monday crept by, then Tuesday and Wednesday. Thursday was my day off so I let deputies know to call me if they saw him outside. All I could think about was this dog and how I had failed him. I thought he was dead, and that his last days were spent suffering because I made the wrong call. I was taking care of other dogs in the garage when my phone rang. It was a fellow deputy that called.

"Bubba's outside, he's alive but in bad shape."

I raced in the house, got dressed, grabbed the warrant and flew down there. I couldn't technically use my red and blues and siren but I did. If another cop saw me I would just say I was looking for someone that had sped past. I would make something up. I backed it down from 100 mph to 10 mph through town. I got to the house and the other deputy was waiting outside. The owner was outside as well when I pulled up.

I asked him his name and he told me. I asked him if Bubba was his dog and he said, "Yes."

"Turn around and put your hands behind his back. You're under arrest for animal neglect,"

"Why?" he asked.

"Look at that dog, what do you mean why?"

He looked back honestly confused. "He's got cancer. I couldn't afford the vet bill and the dog catcher wouldn't come on state land to put him down and I couldn't do it."

"It's not cancer," I told him. "It's mange, and it doesn't explain why you can see every bone in his body."

I was pissed. I told the other deputy to take him in and that I would be taking Bubba to the vet. Bubba was able to walk/stumble to my car. He didn't want to get in, and growled when I tried to pick him up. He didn't have the energy to fight or bite so I put him in the car and drove to the vet. I brought him in and the people in the waiting room all stared. This poor pitiful creature. I explained to the vet it was a neglect case.

"I'm glad you got him," she said.

He was treated for mange and bacterial skin infections. When I got him home I took tons of pictures from every possible angle and light to get the best ones I could. I submitted everything and the guy pleaded guilty. I could now find him a home.

I thought he needed to go somewhere down south. I would get him healthy and send him off. I took him to get groomed and the person did it for free and gave him a bandanna to wear. After a few follow up visits to the vet and a lot of food and water, he was doing better. In the spring I would take him for walks in the woods and he loved it. He loved being free and able to walk where he wanted to. I learned how far we could walk and that he was heavy to carry back if we went too far. He had settled in. Breakfast was now at 9 a.m. or so, and dinner was ALWAYS at 6 p.m. At 5:50 p.m. he would start barking and hobbling around in a circle. At ten past six he would keep circling and come stare in my face. It was time for dinner, dammit.

I looked into homes down south, but how could I be sure they would spoil him to death? Things are getting harder for him. Harder to get up, harder to walk, harder to hear. If I'm not home at six for a feeding, he pees on the bottle of pee cleaner, or something of mine. The thing is, he's still happy. His tail still wags and he can still get up. I'm going to spoil him until that tail isn't wagging anymore.

Bubba's story is why rescue matters, and why advocating for tighter animal cruelty and neglect laws matters. Without tougher laws, dogs like Bubba suffer for years and no one can do anything to stop it.

CHAPTER SIX

The Deputy's Dogs

Keith looks like the type of guy that could lift a pickup truck off a trapped civilian. He's a man's man with a sturdy build and a thick beard that you'd think would translate into more hair on his head, but you'd be wrong. If Keith walked toward me in a parking lot late at night I'd consider emptying my can of pepper spray.

Given his intimidating stature and beard that could frighten a baby, it's a miracle any dog or puppy trusts him at all, but they do. His external look doesn't fit the mold of a traditional caregiver, but the gentle pats on the head, the soothing baths over infected skin, and his reassuring voice turns them all into tail wagging, face licking puppies in no time.

Before his stint as a prison guard, Keith spent his early years working in the roughest parts of south side Chicago repossessing cars in the projects.

> I've been picked up, slammed on the hood of the car then thrown on the curb. I've been *accidentally* kicked, then heeled on with the back of my neck with my face on the pavement. I was racially profiled because I was white and around the projects at two

in the morning. That was why I would get pulled over. I got beat up because of asking questions like, why did I get pulled over? Don't you need my consent to search? What about my fourth amendment rights? I learned after a few times to stop asking those questions and just let them do what they wanted.

I was surprised to learn that his early encounters with law enforcement weren't amicable and that he'd been at the wrong end of a fist more than once from the very officers sworn to protect him. Now, decades later, Keith is the epitome of an officer you'd want protecting your community. I asked Keith about his parents. What he told me was as shocking as it was tragic.

I had just turned eighteen when my dad died of a heart attack. My mom wasn't strong enough to deal with reality. She started drinking. Mom drank herself to death four long and troublesome years later. I was going to join the marines before she died but I stayed back to take care of her. I sold vacuum cleaners door to door. After that I repo'd cars and got into some real sketchy situations.

Sketchy situations that he played out for me like a movie on the big screen. Fast-paced and action-packed with guns, stolen cars and a big payout if you make it back alive with one of those repossessed vehicles. Because he worked for years in the most underserved neighborhoods, Keith experienced what it felt like to be a minority. He learned firsthand about their real life struggles. Everything he'd experienced in his life made his compassion and deep level of kindness toward every living being make sense.

He doesn't look like the type of guy who'd been "talked to" by the Chief, about picking up puppies and putting them in his patrol car, but that's exactly the type of guy he is. Keith was on duty when the message came through the TMAR Facebook page.

If you don't come pick up this puppy, I'll have to call the dog catcher. It wandered into my yard and I can't keep it. I have too many I can't feed already.

Still on duty, but with no action in the hills, Keith decided to sneak over and pick up the unwanted puppy before the dogcatcher would have no choice. The plan was to quickly drop the puppy off at home before any duty calls came in.

Keith set the scared Husky pup with icy blue eyes on the back seat of his patrol car. Between them was plexiglass smeared with muddy paws and snotty nose prints, making it apparent to anyone who'd been back there that his vehicle had carried more dogs than criminals.

All I could think about was, please don't let me get a call, please don't let me get a call.

But a call did come in. A vehicle pursuit. Keith ran to the trunk of his car, pulled out a blanket and his duffel bag, and propped them around the scared pup so he wouldn't get tossed about in the chase. He sped off to meet up with the other officers who were in full pursuit. When he got there a car was in the ditch and the driver was being apprehended. It was Keith's turn to take him in. Another deputy walked the man in handcuffs over to Keith's car for the exchange.

"He can't come with me," Keith was forced to admit. "I don't have room. I've got a puppy in the back."

Because few humans on earth can resist the appeal of a puppy, criminals included, Keith and the two men strolled to the back window and looked in on the fluffy passenger who'd just been on a high speed ride. From underneath the blanket a little black and white head popped out. Two blue eyes stared up at the curious men peering in. A curled tail began to wag. Keith looked at the other men, shrugged his shoulders and said, "I had to take him. Lady was going to call the dog catcher."

· · ·

On a coffee break at the local gas station, the girls behind the counter told Keith they had seen a big brown dog running along the side of Highway 5. Everyone knew if no one picked him up he'd eventually get hit.

Keith took his coffee to go and drove along the blustery highway until he spotted the brown bear-like dog that was running along the gravel shoulder. He stopped his patrol car, got out and threw some treats. Hesitantly, Brown Bear dog ate them up. When Keith tried to inch closer, he would turn and run, trotting scared along the side of the highway with cars racing by. Keith jumped back in his car and followed. He stopped and tried the same technique again and the same thing happened. For thirty minutes the cycle of stop, eat, run, went on. The cold wind continued to blow across the highway in gusts, and the cars never stopped rushing by.

There was no way this dog was going to let Keith touch him or leash him, let alone put him in the back of his car. Keith knelt down and gave every last ounce of patience he had to this deathly scared soul who was furry and big, but underneath, was emaciated. Brown Bear had been on his own for a while, weeks at least. He was starving and the only hope Keith had to get him in his car was if there were no loud noises, no sudden interruptions, and to just keep appealing to this big boy's appetite. Which worked well enough for a while, until it didn't.

So I'm trying to get close enough to slip a leash around his neck but he's really scared, and cars are going by and all I'm thinking is please don't get a call. There would have been nothing I could have done for him. I'd have had to go. He would have either been hit by a car or run off in the woods and starve or freeze to death. I had to do what I had to do. I had to get him. You see this is rescue in the trenches. There isn't always time to gain their trust, let them come to you. There's just not time and if you want to save them, sometimes it's not pretty and it traumatizes them. I hate doing it. Hate hate hate it, but if I didn't, the alternative is worse.

When I got close enough and he was distracted with treats, I knew I had to grab him. I didn't want to, but it was the only way. I figured I'd get bit. He was so scared. In a perfect world, one would have ample time to let that dog trust you, put a lead around him and gently coax him with treats, but there wasn't any time for that. Inevitably, a call would come in and I'd have to go. The moment I grabbed the fur on the back of his neck, his mouth shot forward and his teeth sunk into my inner thigh. Half inch from my, you know. Not kidding, half inch. But I had to just hold on. I grabbed all sixty pounds of dog by the waist and the scruff of the neck and picked him up. He let go of my thigh and I managed to get the car door open and get him inside. After I dropped him off, I had calls so I went on them with blood soaking through my pants until later when I was able to tape a paper towel on my leg.

The dog became known as Chance. He was extremely malnourished and had been severely abused. He wanted nothing to do with humans. Uttering a one syllable word would cause him so much stress he trembled and peed at Keith's feet.

On the same day Keith was tracking down Chance and trying to gain his trust, I was four hours south sitting in my living room, feet kicked up with a glass of wine. After dinner, as I often do, I took out my laptop and started writing. On a bad writing night, I switch over to Facebook and get sucked in like a vacuum has just swallowed me whole and trapped me inside—which is exactly what happened on this night.

A video came across my news feed and caught my attention. It was a brown bear-like dog, body full of winter fur but obviously in bad condition. He hung his head so low his nose almost touched the ground. His mannerisms and tail showed how defeated his spirit was. Then a man's voice came across, "It's okay. I'm not going to hurt you." It was a kind, persistent voice that eventually brought Brown Bear in close enough for a little pet on the head. I don't think I'd ever seen a dog so scared. Yet still there was a tiny movement of his tail and flicker in his eye as he accepted a crumb of kindness. My heart bled for this broken soul.

I'd never heard of Turtle Mountain Animal Rescue or Keith Benning or even about the behemoth problem that existed a few hours away from me. I didn't know that in just a month's time, I'd be meeting the kind voice who showed Brown Bear such compassion. Nor could I have imagined that in just a few years, I'd be part of an organization that would change the lives of thousands of dogs, or that I would take on one very special case myself and never let her go.

Chance's Story

Chance was resilient. It was only a short time before he was jumping and playing with other dogs and learning to trust people. When the video of Chance was posted on the TMAR Facebook page, a friend of Keith's who lived in Colorado reached out. Chance hitched a ride to Colorado and now lives where life is good and green. I reached out to his family, Bill and Jeanna, at the G&G Ranch to see how he is doing today.

"He is extremely happy, well adjusted, and not chewing up the house anymore (his nickname is Chewy.) We named him Charlie, aka, Charles Barkley because he's a bit loud at times. He turned out to be such a great dog. Tell Keith again, thanks for the strange way it all worked out."

This is the video of Keith and Chance that came across my news feed on that serendipitous night. bit.ly/chancethebrownbear

CHAPTER SEVEN

An Angel is Born

Grand Forks, North Dakota- Aliah Chappell

"I was watching the news and saw a story of how Keith and his wife were rescuing dogs up by the Belcourt area. Having lived by the Spirit Lake Reservation and knowing how bad the dog problem can be, I instantly had tremendous respect for them. I decided to look up Turtle Mountain Animal Rescue on Facebook then started following the page.

One night before going to bed I was on Facebook and there was this DESPERATE plea for help. Basically the post said if people don't step up and start helping, Keith and his wife were going to be done. They couldn't financially or physically keep doing what they were doing.

You could tell they were at their end. I don't know how to describe it, but the post was written kind of . . . scary? Like an angry email you'd get from your boss. It just sounded so real. I'd followed other animal rescue pages but this post stuck out to me. This was real life. These two people needed help and they were only three hours away from where I lived.

I made a donation but I still didn't feel better. I lay in bed and kept thinking about them for the next few days. I just couldn't forget about it. I was wearing a sweatshirt I had bought from a Bonfire campaign that supported Family Dogs New Life Shelter in Oregon where we had gotten our dog.

That's when it clicked.

I was like, well why don't I reach out to TMAR and see if they would want me to make a T-shirt on Bonfire? We could raise some money for them that way. I did some research and it seemed simple enough, just make a T-shirt, promote it on-line, Bonfire does all the work and TMAR gets the money. I sent TMAR a message and got a quick response from Keith. He was like, yes, absolutely. Let's do this."

...

And so . . . an angel was born.

More were on the way. Together they would help keep TMAR stay afloat through the burnout hell everyone before them had crumbled under. Up to that point, no other volunteers besides Aliah, had stickability. To succeed long-term in rescue work you have to have an incredible amount of self-motivation, passion and a whole lotta' fall-down-get-back-up in you. Even more, you have to be a little bit crazy. It is common in the rescue world for volunteers to readily admit that they, along with their comrades, all have one or more screws loose.

Because this statement outs me as one of the crazies too, I must admit that it's true. Upon further examination, the crazy factor actually means animal rescue attracts *those that are uncustomary*. Individuals that are willing to sacrifice their time and money otherwise spent on lavish American commodities to give back instead of consume. Rescue work is tumultuous at best, fatiguing at the very least. Friendships are tested, marriages stressed, hearts broken and former lives dissolve under the sometimes oppressive duties that come with saving animals no one else wants. Only the toughest people survive this type of selfless life.

Aliah fits the mold and was one of just a few volunteers that stuck around long enough to make a difference. She and her husband just had their first baby around the time she reached out to Keith. Aliah was a full-time nurse and mom, but still, she couldn't turn away from what was happening so close to her. She found moments to help, sometimes one minute, sometimes an hour. She was notorious for sneaking into the bathroom at work to return messages or help line up transports.

I asked her to tell me about those early days when she'd just met Keith. This is what she said.

"Turns out there was a couple of problems. One, I have zero experience with Photoshop and designing T-shirts. And two, Keith, I would soon learn, is EXTREMELY PICKY. I put together a tacky looking shirt with the clip art images that Bonfire supplied (a paw print of course) with the TMAR name on it. It was seriously awful. Then Keith kept going on and on about how he wanted it to have a dream catcher with the words intertwined and blah blah blah and I was in way over my head. I needed help. I wanted it to be perfect so we could raise some good money for these folks and the animals. My husband said why don't you ask Jennie? She does graphic design and could probably help you out. So I messaged her, she was in. I introduced her to Keith and in a few days she had a shirt made with our ND rescue design and the most perfect quote on the back.

We launched the fundraiser and three to four days in had already brought in one thousand dollars profit (I think that doubled whatever was in the TMAR account at that time) whenever I wore the shirt I got asked constantly where I got it from.

I kept in touch with Keith over Facebook and started doing transports here and there, then I went down for a rummage sale in Belcourt later that summer where all the profits would benefit TMAR. We made four hundred bucks at that rummage sale! That was the day I met Keith in person.

Keith asked me if I could take back a couple of dogs with me. The Muppets I called them. A family with two young kids were giving up their beloved dogs because they couldn't afford to buy them food or take care of them. They cried when they put them in my car. I cried on the way home thinking about it. These people loved these dogs but just couldn't afford them. I know this is judging, but the way they looked, they could probably barely afford to feed the kids too.

I went home and had a reality check. The Muppets stayed at my house overnight. It was my first foster I guess you could say. I gave them baths, bought them new collars then I brought them to a shelter where they would eventually be adopted. Knowing what I do now, I had such a different way of thinking back then. I learned to not judge people who give up their animals. The Muppets were given up out of love. They have a better life now because of the selflessness of that family. After that day I was hooked, I wanted to keep helping TMAR."

. . .

In rescue especially, emotions run high, stress is ever present and tension can begin to unravel even the best of friendships and happiest of marriages. Hours of transporting barking, crying puppies and dogs, endless trips to the vet, fostering in addition to having your own animals, makes for a life that is far from normal. Volunteering in animal rescue is a noble, selfless act. Rarely does anyone have ample time and money to do the work they do without tremendous personal sacrifice. This is what Keith's life had become. He needed help with every aspect of the rescue operations. One by one he amassed a small but mighty team that evolved together and overcame the impossible. Keith dubbed that team The Angels and another one was about to be born.

*Jennie was with TMAR for about two years after that first T-shirt project. She played a pivotal role in fund raising, fostering, transport coordination, rescue-to-rescue relations and more. She was involved with many aspects of the daily rescue operations. Jennie eventually left TMAR, but continued her rescue efforts with multiple organizations. She still saves lives today. I reached out to Jennie and asked if she wanted to tell me about her time with the TMAR, she gave me permission to use her real name but declined to comment further.

Smokey's Story

Her whiskers were scorched and her hair was covered in soot when the firemen found her. Smokey was the sole survivor of a house fire that destroyed everything around her.

The Belcourt Fire Department responded to a house engulfed in flames. After putting out the fire, a two-hour search showed no signs of people or animals dead or alive. On a routine follow-up the next day, they found Smokey. The firemen sifted through the ash and rubble looking for a lingering spark when Smokey stepped out from underneath what was left of the deck. She was scared but not injured. The other dog she was with did not survive.

"No one really knew what to do [about Smokey]. Everyone already had too many animals. I had known Keith Benning from working with him when he was at the Sheriff's office," Dylan Medrud said. "I told the boys he does great work and I trust him and his organization. They agreed and we contacted him."

That is how Smokey came to TMAR. This story might seem insignificant if you live in a city with animal control, where firemen or officers can take foundlings. But here, before

Keith turned his life and home into an animal rescue, there were few, if any, good options for dogs like Smokey.

Thank you to Aj Laducer, Lerrik Gourneau (pictured holding Smokey), Kole Poitra (also pictured) and Dylan Stuart Medrud for your service and compassion toward animals. Photo courtesy from the firemen at the Belcourt Fire Department.

CHAPTER EIGHT

Angels Get Wings

Manitoba, Canada –Trista Zacharias

"I had been following TMAR for a couple of months. I often commented or liked things on the page. One evening I received a message from Keith, a complete stranger to me. He explained who he was and asked if I would be willing to help manage the

Facebook page and assist in setting up some transports.

I didn't hesitate for a second! Shortly after becoming involved we received a message about a dog that had been beaten with a bat. After that another story came in of a sweet golden-colored pup. Her fur was patchy and green from having paint and bleach thrown on her by children. The pictures were so hard to see. The dogs coming in and the stories that followed them were often so depressing. I knew that my help was needed so badly even though I wanted to scream and cry and be so angry for the suffering these animals endured.

At the time I was eight months pregnant, Keith was running on empty. He sent me a long message explaining that he wasn't sure he could continue doing what he was doing with so little help. I cried for three days straight. I couldn't sleep wondering what would happen if Keith stepped away. Who would be there to pick up the pieces and care for the animals?"

. . .

Keith told Trista and Aliah about a grant he found that TMAR might qualify for. If they were awarded the grant, it would be enough money to build a shelter and cover operating costs for a long time. It would be exactly what they needed to succeed where no one had before.

At the time Aliah and Trista teamed up with Keith there were a few hundred bucks in a GoFundMe account and a few hundred followers watching their efforts on Facebook. Nearly all of the rescue expenses such as dog food and supplies, vet bills and transportation came out of Keith's pocket, the pockets of a few volunteers, and a handful of donors. They *had* to get that grant money. It would mean the difference between continuing or going broke.

There were a few problems. None of them had ever applied for a grant before. In fact, no one had ever done any kind of fundraising before. In order to even qualify for the grant, TMAR would have to show they had ten thousand dollars in the bank. No one knew how to raise ten thousand dollars or if it was even possible. There were obstacles to overcome. For example, there was no local money that could be raised. The very county they were trying to serve had nothing more to give. The state had nothing available for them either. When it came to doling out government funds for animal welfare the officials at every level seemed to turn into ghosts.

When we first started doing rescue I went to everyone. I started with the cities but they said it was the county's problem or the tribe's. Nobody had the money, or at least they were not going to spend the money. When you live in the second poorest county in the state it's hard to get money, especially for animals. The county did eventually offer to get us a grant for a shelter, but the price was too high and it was too much of a risk. They would own the building; they would lease it to us and charge a fee. We could pay rent each month, but then we are at the whim of future politicians that may or may not support our cause. What happens when the next group of politicians gets voted in? Do they raise the rent? Make new rules? Cancel our lease? If we were going to do it, we were going to do it right so that the animals always have a place to go.

I originally met with the tribe and that didn't go anywhere either. We took dogs from the dog catchers so they didn't have to shoot them. We had a meeting, came up with plans, but it was never followed through. The new council has agreed to law changes but that has yet to happen.

Beating down dead end doors became a waste of time and energy. Keith and the Angels were better off going grassroots, boots on the ground, creating a system of the people, by the people, for the people and the animals. Waiting on someone else to do something or a government entity and all its red tape to step in would take too long. Dogs were dying, suffering by the hundreds each year. Thousands more would perish in the coming winters while politicians sat on their hands the way they have done regarding animal welfare for decades. There was no more time for inaction.

Keith's choice to create something from nothing would prove to be the right choice and go on to save countless lives, but not without cost and consequence.

In order to raise enough money and get good help consistently and permanently, the team would have to overcome their status as nobodies in nowhere land. Who is going to give money to a garage rescue in the middle of nowhere that no one has ever heard of? Keith who? Where? You mean on the reservation? The team encountered daily objections like, "I'm not going to give my money to the reservation." But they were undeterred.

Rescue Recipe
-Mix together motivated women hell-bent on saving animals
-Pour in one dash of unstoppable dude
-Watch miracles happen

Keith and the Angels began to fly.

It was no small feat and took many months, but between the Bonfire T-shirt campaign, the rummage sale, and an online raffle where they sold donated items, the team of newbie crusaders actually pulled it off. They raised *more* than ten thousand dollars.

For months and months and months they did everything they could. When they did the raffle, they

raised more than what we needed for the grant. I
really thought the grant was the answer. I knew that
if we applied for it, we would get it, and then we
could build a shelter. I really thought that was going
to be it for us.

I asked Aliah about that grant and what happened next.
"Keith was so excited, he couldn't believe we raised the money!
We couldn't believe we raised the money! He really thought
that was going to be the ticket. But when we went to apply for
the grant, it was gone. It had been pulled and was no longer
available. Keith was absolutely devastated. I thought he was
going to throw in the towel. I really did think it was all going to
be over."

. . .

Word was out. They were a real rescue. They raised money
and had volunteers from around the state pitching in to help.
The dozens of animals Keith was taking each month, and the
handful of messages he used to get each day was peanuts in
comparison to what was happening now. The perception to
some of the locals was that TMAR was turning a profit off of
the dogs, confirming their suspicions that the rescue was just a
cover to get rich. Never mind that the Benning's personal debt
from vet bills alone, was crippling. Yet still, they didn't take
one dollar from any of the money raised to pay themselves
back, nor did they take any type of wage for their round-the-
clock work.

When messages came in asking for help with strays, it
didn't matter that there was no real shelter, that it was still just
Keith and his wife, a garage, and a few volunteers behind the

scenes. If they didn't respond right away or weren't able to pick up the next litter of stray pups (it didn't matter if it was the fifth litter of the day) the legitimacy of what they were doing was continually questioned. People were always suspicious. *Were they just making money and not actually rescuing dogs? Was TMAR a total scam?*

Someone posted on a local online garage sale page that they had a litter of puppies they were trying to find homes for. When another person suggested they contact TMAR for help their response was, *I'd rather call the dogcatcher than give these dogs to them so they can make money.*

Unfortunately, this sentiment was not isolated.

Some people didn't want to see us succeed, even in rescuing dogs. Some people just don't like to see good things happen on the reservation. The people that live here will agree that happens. I don't know if it's jealousy or just that they want everyone else to be as miserable as they are.

We had people call the state and complain about something they made up. It was all a lie. Someone approached the tribe and tried to ban us from rescuing dogs on tribal land. The most common sabotage still today is people making up fake stories about us stealing dogs, which isn't the case.

Gossip and accusations added to the stress and feelings of burnout the small team faced daily. "They are taking our dogs and selling them for profit," was the most prevalent word vomit that circulated. A statement that proved whoever propagated it knew nothing about what the team was doing. If they did, they would have known there was no money made on selling the rescued dogs. TMAR did not sell or adopt out dogs, TMAR only rescued them—a business model that spent money but had no reliable source of income coming in. The accusations of stealing and using the dog problem for profit were a slap in the face for everyone involved. The volunteers of TMAR didn't want or need recognition, and they certainly didn't deserve that type of condemnation.

Keith took in the worst-of-the-worst medical cases in addition to surrendered pets and the never-ending unwanted litters. Then he made sure those animals went to a safe place where they could be adopted. There was not a cent to be made from this type of rescue, only a life's savings to be lost. A small amount of money came in from donations by people who believed in the cause. Most of the money that funded the daily operation was put in by Keith himself and the volunteers. No one touched the money the Angels raised for the grant. They set that money aside with the hope that one day they could raise enough to build a shelter.

The Bennings moved to a larger house with two bedrooms on the outskirts of town. The address still remains unknown and Keith has to protect that privacy like a first-born child, or risk his personal residence turning into a dumping ground for unwanted animals. Attached to his home is a pole-barn type garage—a man's garage that was meant to hold tools, trucks, tractors, and other man-stuff men accumulate. Instead, Keith's cave quickly turned into temporary housing for not just hundreds, but eventually thousands of animals. Animals that displaced all the man stuff that had to be moved somewhere else to make room. On my first visit to Keith's garage rescue I saw exactly where all that man stuff went—in one corner, piled high. Very high.

Keith's new garage was immediately transformed into rescue central. A small operation with four large wire kennels meant to temporarily hold animals until he could find a real shelter to take them. Inside the house there is a wood burning fireplace in the main living room, a floor fan is fastened in the doorway that blows heat into the garage so the dogs don't freeze. His personal washer and dryer ran twenty-four hours a day cleaning soiled towels and his kitchen sink became a place to bathe puppies. His entire house turned into a makeshift animal shelter. The history of the home itself is like a page from the handbook of a religious cult or a scene from the *Blair Witch Project*, too dark and creepy to retell here.

> The surrounding land is beautiful but the water quality from the well is terrible. I have to dump bleach pellets down the well three times a year just to cut down on some of the smell. I put in a house filter and a softener, but the water is still barely drinkable. On a good week I can give the dogs straight tap water but on a bad week I mix half and half with bottled water out of five gallon jugs, or straight bottled water.

There were more animals coming in than their new house could hold and the inevitable soon happened. A garage full of dogs spilled into a house full of dogs.

Dogs like Lucas.

164.165.166.167.168.169.170.171.172.173.174.
175.176.177.178.179.180.181.182.183.184.185.
186.187.188.189.190.191.192.193.194.195.196.
197.198.199.200.201.202.203.204.205.206.207.
208.209.210.211.212.213.214.215.216.217.218.
219.220.221.222.223.224.225.226.227.228.229.
230.231.232.233.234.235.236.237.238.239.240.
241.242.243.244.245.246.247.248.249.250.251.
252.253.254.255.256.257.258.259.260.261.262.
263.264.265.266.267.268.269.270......................

....

....

....

....

....

....

....

....

....

....998.

Lucas's Story

Someone reported to the police that a vicious pit bull had attacked their family dog and was still hanging around on the porch. Keith was on duty that night and dispatched to check the scene.

When I walked up to the porch his head was split wide open. It was like an open zipper to his skull. His head was full of blood. Someone messed this dog up bad, I thought. This was not just a dog fight. I talked nice to him and his tail wagged. He put his head down and I slipped a leash around him.

He'd gotten into a fight with the resident dog over food because he was totally starving. He was a fur colored skeleton with cuts and bite marks all over. Someone hit him over the head with a shovel or something. He was a total mess. He is going to cost a lot of money to save I thought. How are we going to afford this? We can't.

The other cop looked at me and said, "You want me to do it or you want to do it?"

The dog just sat there at my side, looked up at me and wagged his tail. He looked like he was saying

Keith, "please help me." I couldn't do it. I just couldn't do it.

I threw a blanket over the back seat and took him home. He was in so much pain that night. I used steri-strips and duct tape to patch up his head. I had no idea what I was doing and his wounds were bad. I frankensteined him up with gauze and hugs and did the best I could. An ER vet bill would've been at least three hundred dollars and we were already thousands in debt to the vet.

Lucas didn't have an ounce of aggression through anything I did to him and this dog was in SO much pain. He cried all night long. He didn't want outside, it was just an *I hurt* cry. I didn't sleep for more than a few minutes at a time that night. I got up to go comfort him, then I'd go back to bed and he'd cry again. He just wanted someone to stay with him.

I called a vet in Grand Forks that night and she said she'd be there at 7:30 a.m. to come out and see him. Grand Forks is nearly three hours away but she showed up at seven-thirty on the dot and brought him back with her to the clinic. She stitched him up, fixed his broken teeth, and took care of him.*

Tonya, one of the foster coordinators at No Dog Left Behind, a canine rescue in Brooklyn Center, Minnesota (eight hours from where Lucas was found) agreed to take him in. I reached out to them looking for an update on where he is today. I was delighted to find him.

Tonya and the crew at NDLB had never seen or read the article about Lucas that was published in the Grand Forks Herald while he was under vet care there. She also didn't know the details about how Keith came to find Lucas that night. All she knew was that he was in bad shape and had come from a world that was cruel to him. Tears were shed between us as we exchanged messages about his harrowing journey.

Tonya took Lucas into her home about two years ago, and as I write this today, he has never left her family. Lucas is still up for adoption. When I found that out, I was shocked. Why wasn't he adopted?! She told me he loves kids, is good with other dogs, but probably wouldn't do well with cats. She said he is well-mannered and house trained. Lucas is a totally normal, perfect, lovable family dog.

But I knew exactly why Lucas had not been moved along the rescue chain. Lucas is branded with a stigma that plagues his entire breed—a stigma that keeps dogs like him from being adopted. Dogs like Lucas are sentenced to death in shelters across the United States in unconscionable numbers because of two words.

Pit bull.

The statistics on how many pit bull-type dogs, labeled Pit Mix or Pit X, that go into shelters and never come out, leave me gasping for air. Exact statistics vary from agency to agency but it's safe to say that 20 percent of all dogs going into shelters are labeled Pit Mix and of those dogs, 40 percent don't make it out alive. A stark contrast from the Labrador retriever who has an estimated seven percent kill-rate after entering a shelter, and the German shepherd at just two percent. There is an unfounded discrimination against pit bull looking dogs that is the reason for the massive chasm between which dogs live and which die.

This is what Tonya said about Lucas. "Some of the other ladies in the rescue believe that Lucas "sabotages" his meet and greets because he loves living with me. Honestly, I don't mind having him around. I am a huge advocate for the breed and work towards removing the stigma that comes when someone hears the words pit bull. Lucas and I are snuggle buddies, he loves to lounge on the sofa and watch TV, but I better be rubbing his belly too, or he'll make sure to let me know that I'm forgetting something by nudging or pawing at my arm. He absolutely adores children and he has a blast with most of the other foster dogs that come through my house. He has learned to sit, shake, down and stay. He is really good at all of them! Lucas has become a favorite of the crew at NDLB and we are all very protective of him and continue to search far and wide for his forever family."

There you have it. Another dog well taken care of but stuck in the system of foster and adoption.

Lucas is why adopt-don't-shop matters.

Buying animals from pet stores and breeding dogs to bring more of them into a world that cannot take care of their brothers and sisters, keeps millions of dogs like Lucas stuck in the system or sentenced to death. A friend once told me that if I bought a dog it would sentence seven other shelter dogs to death. I was curious to see if that was just rhetoric or if those statistics were close to the truth. I dug in to find out. What I wanted to know was, *does buying a dog sentence other shelter dogs to death?* The answer I found was yes. Yes it does.

45 million: households in the U.S. that have a dog.

1.5 million: of those homes have a rescued dog.

43.5 million: households have dogs that were intentionally brought into the world.

Of those 43.5 million homes that have bought dogs, if ONE out of every sixty-four families adopted a dog *instead*, it would END euthanasia for dogs in shelters across United States.

3 million: dogs go into shelters in the U.S. each year.

1.5 million: of those shelter dogs get adopted.

670,000: dogs get euthanized because they did not get adopted, are deemed unadoptable, or there is simply just, no room.

Ending euthanasia of healthy unwanted dogs is a problem that is solvable and within our grasp. A rescue revolution has begun. Through awareness, education, and encouraging one another to adopt not shop, we can end the suffering of millions of homeless dogs right now. Not in twenty years, not in the next generation, right now. If we do nothing, we sentence dogs waiting in shelters to death, and the next ones in line for that kennel share the same fate, and the next and the next.

If you're interested in reading the article about Lucas and watching the video that was published in a local paper, I've included it here.
http://bit.ly/LucasVideoGFHerald

No Dog Left Behind can be found here. https://www.ndlbrescue.org/

*Although I wanted to give recognition to the vet who helped Lucas, this individual asked to remain anonymous.

**Hal Herzog Ph.D., The Puzzling Geography of Animal Shelter Dog Euthanasia, a new study examines the cruel geography of deaths in animal shelters. https://www.psychologytoday.com/us/blog/animals-and-us/201805/the-puzzling-geography-animal-shelter-dog-euthanasia

CHAPTER NINE

Dogs Because People Suck

(Daisy)

There is no shortage of memes and T-shirts illustrating why the animal kingdom is superior to the human race, because there is no shortage of cruelty, neglect and loathsome behavior toward animals. All Lucas wanted was food and a warm house because that is the very nature of dogs. Perhaps if we had a better understanding of the domestic dog and its natural place in our families, fewer humans would consider them *just a dog.*

The word domesticated is derived from the phrase *of the house.* Dogs grew up alongside humans, in our hearts and in our homes. They are not wolves that can fend for themselves. They are *domesticated* dogs we helped to create.

The first wolf-would-be-dogs were taken into the home thousands of years before any other animal. They evolved initially through self-domestication. Wolves that were tamer than the others got food. The wolves who walked in with their heads low and a passive demeanor were allowed near the villages, and offered basic protection. It was those wolves who survived during harsher times. Those tame wolf-dogs continued to breed, passing along traits humans preferred.

Later, through human intervention in the gene pool, wolf dogs were fashioned and molded through selective breeding, eventually becoming the modern dogs we have today.

Although dogs and wolves share extraordinarily similar DNA, dogs do not express the same genes as their wild ancestors. Traits wolves possess that allow them to thrive in the wild are not turned on in dogs. Contrary to what sensationalized media coverage has reported, a pack of dogs does not act like a pack of wolves. Even feral dogs over many generations do not revert back to a wolf pack. They stay near the town. They act as scavengers, not sophisticated, coordinated pack hunters. It is possible some of the same genes that are expressed in wolves are expressed in some dogs, but it would take thousands of years of evolution and selective pressure to force domesticated dogs back into a more wolf-like genetic make-up.

Wolves are wolves.

Dogs are dogs.

Dogs are part of the house. Wolves are part of the wild kingdom. For the modern dog, the ability to fend for itself has been bred out over millennia. We have shaped and molded the dogs that live alongside us. Effectively, we've conditioned them to depend on the house for shelter and the family unit for survival. Our ancestors assisted in the evolution of turning wild wolves into dogs some ten thousand, maybe hundreds of thousands of years ago.* In doing so, they passed down to us the responsibility to care for them. Dogs are a gift from our ancestors of long ago.

The world is waking up. There are more of us now than ever before that understand dogs require the essentials any other member of the family requires. We are at the tipping point where more people than not understand it's our responsibility to be good stewards. This moral trend has gained momentum and doesn't seem to be slowing down. I am optimistic about the future.

Since the 1970s there has been a steady decline in the euthanasia rates of companion animals in shelters. Partly because there has been a major cultural shift in how we think about our pets. They weren't always the embedded family members most of us know them to be today. Animal welfare advocates have crusaded across the nation over the last four decades and have successfully changed hearts and minds. There has been a dramatic shift toward the acceptance of dogs as domesticated family members instead of treating them as a thing to be discarded.

This national mindshift is a huge win for the animals and is evident by the drop of euthanasia rates in shelters. But the work is not done. The individuals who advocate for animals by using their voice and their consumer power is still too small. To solve the pandemic of companion animal suffering across the globe, will require more individuals to stop talking and take action. One simple action, adopt don't shop.

A lot of people say "I love animals" and of course they do. They love their family pets and care when they see a creature in duress, I do too. However, for a few others, there is something more profound within us than just feeling empathy for animals. We feel a stronger connection to the animal kingdom that goes beyond pet ownership and just a general respect. We are the advocates—the individuals who not only care, but do something about it. More of us are needed to make a global change.

. . .

About the time Keith realized the place he'd moved to had a problem that was out of control the likes of which he'd never seen, I'd just published my first book. To my surprise, my unexpected project had some unexpected success. Since then, I've learned that this is how my writing career goes. I don't pick the project, the project picks me, and once it does, it doesn't leave me alone until it's done.

In 2015, I filled out an online job application to be a writer for PETA (People for the Ethical Treatment of Animals). The organization people love to hate. Either way, they have done a tremendous amount of work to end suffering across multiple industries that have exploited animals for decades. Their willingness to be a little crazy with their tactics is what attracted me. They declined to take a serious look at my application. I usually persist and try to find another way in, but on this endeavor, I just gave up. I shrugged my shoulders and moved on without knowing why my usually undeterred attitude didn't prevail. Had I known then, what I know now about PETA, I would have pounded down their door and tried a lot harder to make them realize that I could be an asset.** But at that time, something inside me just knew it wasn't quite right. Over the next three years I found a home for my skills in a place that needed my help far more than PETA ever would.

My husband used to tell me to volunteer at the humane society, help walk dogs, do this, do that. All of that is great, but none of it ever *called* to me. Nothing ever jumped out, reached in, grabbed my heart and swallowed it whole.

Until it did.

---

*The exact evolutionary timeline from wolf to dog varies from source to source. The exact moment in history where wolves became dogs is not relevant to the content here.

** TMAR rescued thousands of animals over the coming years. PETA was the only worldwide animal rights organization that offered assistance and didn't turn them away in times of desperate need. PETA has been an ally to TMAR when others have closed their doors.

John Doe Dog

 I saved a little mange puppy one time. He was skin and bones and running through town. A drunk guy had picked him up and was carrying him. I was too busy on calls to go check on him but later that night I saw the puppy on the side of the road. I pulled over and he crept up towards me, wagged his tail, then got startled and ran into the road.

I watched him get run over. I went over to him and I knew there was no way he would make it. I was helpless to do anything, it was horrible. I picked him up and put him in my patrol car. I drove to the church parking lot and sat with him in the grass. He wasn't in much pain by then, the damage was inside. I held him and petted him as he passed. That was all I could do.

I beat myself up for doing it all wrong, making that happen. I took him home and buried him that night. I couldn't cry because you can't cry and do rescue like this and still function. You have to save all your emotional energy for waking up the next morning and doing it all over again.

CHAPTER TEN

A Cold Surrender

I believe luck is preparation
meeting opportunity.
-Oprah Winfrey

I'd been waiting for it, preparing for it, even though I didn't know what *it* was going to be. As it often does, the right opportunity presented itself at the right time. I guess you could say it was luck.

A friend I hadn't seen in a while posted on Facebook that she was transporting rescue dogs. It was a picture of some tiny puppies riding in her back seat. I sent her a message saying that I'd be interested in helping her sometime if she needed someone to ride shotgun, or perhaps I could ride in the back next to those puppies—just saying. A few weeks later Brenda messaged me back and invited me with her to a surrender event. I had no idea what a surrender event was, but she said we'd save dogs and I just had a feeling that what Brenda was doing might be exactly what I'd been waiting for.

That intuition was right. That invitation was the beginning of a new adventure that would transform my life in the years to come—a journey that would take me out of my privileged city and state. What lay ahead left me crying, laughing, soul-searching, and eventually, doing what I wanted to be doing . . . rescuing dogs and writing (and drinking wine.) Like all volunteer work does, it occupied a good chunk of my time and money. I wouldn't have it any other way.

Brenda and I set out on a freezing cold Saturday morning. The sky was midnight blue and I could feel the harsh tundra temperatures on my skin—it was the kind of cold you feel in your bones. I shuffled down my icy driveway toward Brenda's SUV. There was a rectangular magnet displayed on the side. It had a large red emergency cross symbol and the words Animal Rescue Vehicle. I slid into the heated passenger seat where a welcome warmth and the smell of hazelnut coffee enveloped me. The sound of my friend's voice was a sign that I was exactly where I was supposed to be, "You ready to go save some dogs today?"

Yes.

Yes, I was.

Behind my cozy seat stacked neatly from floor to ceiling were different sized wire kennels. Each had its own clean white hospital blanket inside and another draped on the outside separating what would soon be unfamiliar noses riding inches from each other. Over the next four hours I drank coffee and ate Brenda's hard boiled eggs on my way to a place up north that I'd passed through once or twice, almost three decades earlier.

Brenda has short spiky hair that looks wet even when it's dry and I've never seen her wear anything other than a shirt with a slogan about animal rights that oftentimes includes profanity. She wears her deepest convictions about how animals should be treated not just on her sleeve but on her back, her chest, and even tattooed on her skin. Brenda is a Clydesdale, if there are dogs that need help, move out of her way or she may trample you to get to them. Yet she is gentle and one of the most caring souls I've ever met. The perfect person for the job of rescuing humans and animals which is what she does in both her career and personal life.

We arrived in Belcourt, North Dakota, a little town tucked away just below the Canadian border. It was like arriving back in time. The town looked the same as I'd remembered it. My dad grew up not far from here and we'd passed through the area a time or two. There were old buildings in a state of continual disarray, very few local amenities and I got the sense that I was out of place. Unwelcome, perhaps. Like other small towns in North Dakota it felt like the modern world evolved around them, leaving them behind.

We rolled in past the casino and into the parking lot of the local community center. I was looking for stray dogs wandering the street, hanging around corners or curled up in the ditch, but there were none. I didn't see a single dog in need of even one of the kennels stacked behind my seat.

They were invisible.

A quick four hours later, Brenda and I were on our way back to Fargo with fifteen dogs and puppies curled up in warm blankets in those wire crates. Plus, one big husky-shepperdish-mix with her front paws across my lap and her back paws on the floor between my feet. In all, with a dozen or more volunteers, six vehicles overflowing with kennels, and one very large RV gutted and outfitted with many more, we rescued more than seventy unwanted or stray dogs. In four hours.

Mind.

Blown.

It took me an hour of sitting in silence, while I stroked the head of the gentle dog on my lap, to process what I'd just seen. I laced my fingers through her thick winter coat—the coat of a dog who'd lived out doors for many months. She had small patches of dry, black, frost bitten skin on her elbows and ears. Her eyes clear and deep brown, her teeth white and clean, she was a puppy no more than a year old yet had the temperament of a dog who was mature and wise. She lay over me the whole way home, content, not panting, not needy, whiny or with a speck of anxiety. I had enough anxiety for both of us. My mind was reeling with questions and searching for answers.

Why does the problem exist?

How could that land just spit out that many unwanted dogs?

Who else knows about this?

How come I didn't know?

Where is the money from the state to fix this?

Why is there no animal control?

Why isn't anyone doing something!

Dogs are dying out there!!

She answered as many questions as she could. Over many years of volunteering, she had seen and learned a lot, but eventually she told me, "I'm the person on the ground who picks them up, cares for them and makes sure they find a home. I don't do any of that big picture stuff."

All I could think about was that big picture stuff. North Dakota as a whole is wealthy. There are plenty of jobs, the economy is good, and we don't live in the protected economic bubble, we *are* the bubble. I couldn't fathom what I'd just seen or how long it has been going on. Years? Decades? Centuries? The world I thought I knew where dogs suffer some place south of here, in a city I've never heard of, in a place that I could do nothing about except send eighteen dollars month, was shattered.

I couldn't look away from this. There were no excuses to not help and someone *was* doing something. Someone organized that event. Brenda told me who it was and pointed him out while we were there. He was lifting kennels and bags of dog food, carrying supplies and handling dogs no one else could handle. I met his wife, I handed her a small wad of cash and bag of supplies. I thanked her for what they were doing, at that time I had no idea the magnitude of their sacrifice.

My plan was to reach out to them, I had to. I wouldn't be able to sleep at night knowing this was going on in a place so close to me and that I was doing nothing to help. The pilot light in me that had been waiting for action was ignited and the gas was about to be turned up. Way up. After a few days of thinking about what I'd seen I had more questions than ever before.

There was only one person who could answer them.

Band of Brothers

"Trespassers Will Be Shot" was nailed prominently to trees and zip tied to posts in nearly every yard we drove past.

Ten minutes earlier at the community center someone pulled up to surrender a dog they couldn't care for. When the woman opened the car door, the dog took off. Brenda and I watched the dog sprint across the parking lot and through an intersection before disappearing into a residential neighborhood.

I held up a slip lead, "Should we try to get her?" I asked Brenda.

We both knew the chance of finding the dog, then coercing her to come with us was slim but we tried anyway. I slid into Brenda's oversized SUV, secretly welcoming the opportunity to get out of the cold. The green illuminated lights on the dash read minus twenty-three degrees. The glare off the sun and snow was blinding, and there wasn't a cloud in the sky. It seemed like a perfect winter day until you stepped outside. It was hard to imagine that the conditions just beyond the glass were deadly. I wondered what it must be like for the stray dogs out there, or the newborn puppies who have no warmth to escape to. How could they live outside in the cold? I knew the answer.

By some miracle a few survive, but most die.

As we drove slowly through the neighborhood looking for the black and white dog, all I could think about was what if we didn't find her? How could she possibly survive the winter? Where would she sleep? Where would she find food or water? I felt like her life was in our hands. Find her and she lives, drive away and she dies.

It seemed impossible that we'd ever see her again. There were so many places she could be hiding, hunkered down trying not to be seen. Old cars and rusted-out tractors sat dormant in front yards. Storage sheds with open doors were in the back. There were trees, bushes even furniture scattered about. Never mind the "Trespassers Will Be Shot" signs we'd have to navigate if we did find her.

After thirty minutes of looking, we felt we had no choice. We decided to go back to the community center where we could help with the dozens of other dogs people were bringing in from the cold. I reminded Brenda not to turn around in anyone's driveway. The feeling of being out of place and unwelcome was ever-present. We turned around in the street and headed back. That's when I saw them.

A band of brothers lying in the middle of the road adjacent to us. They were sunning themselves, taking an afternoon nap on the snow-covered street. Their thick, lustrous coats protected them from the frozen ground below and the bitter cold air above.

The big white and brown one lifted his head and looked at us—completely unaffected by our presence, not moving or caring if we stayed or drove past. He lay his head back down and resumed his afternoon nap.

I inched to the edge of my seat, closer to the windshield to get a better look. They didn't have collars but I surmised that a family nearby loved them and let them roam because they always came back. I imagined they got food and water each day and maybe even an outdoor doghouse was available when they needed it. Perhaps little kids loved them and once in a while, they got to go inside and snuggle on a bed at night.

We stared at them lying there in the sun on the snowpack. Their winter fur was thick with a white undercoat of many layers like the Siberian Husky I had growing up. These boys were well adapted to the outdoors—the type of dog who prefers to be outdoors. They looked healthy and well fed.

Brenda and I did not talk about these dogs. There was no debate on whether or not we should do something for them. All signs pointed to that someone was looking out for them. Perhaps not in the way big city folk look out for their dogs. They didn't have knitted sweaters, waterproof booties or blinged out collars. These dogs were free to roam and live outside in conditions they were mostly equipped for. These brothers were not the kind of dogs we were there for. We were there for the unwanted and the homeless.

As we drove away, I said to Brenda, "I bet there are a lot of crazy animal fanatics who would try to coax those dogs in." She took a deep frustrated breath and nodded, confirming what I already knew to be true. "That sucks," I said. "People like that give rescue workers like you a bad rap."

"Yes they do."

CHAPTER ELEVEN

The Rescue Writer

I wanted to find out more about the man behind the mission. I stalked him on social media to see what the scoop was on this animal rescuing deputy.

He *seemed* like the real deal. The pictures and videos of the dogs he took into his home were heartbreaking. He was picking up and caring for the animals no one else wanted and established an actual nonprofit rescue organization. Word was, the deputy was also planning to build a shelter. Keith Benning dared to solve a complex and immense problem in a difficult area. He was a visionary.

His mission ignited a spark in me—some dormant energy with an unlimited supply of motivation woke me up. I had to help this underdog—this crazy dude who seemed to believe that he might actually make a dent or even fix this mammoth problem. I reached out to Keith on Facebook. *I want to help. How best can I help you?*

As we talked, I got a sense of the scope and magnitude of what he was dealing with on a daily basis, and the deep-rooted causes and possible solutions. We discussed how factors like poverty and addiction contribute to the problems in the area, human and animal alike. There isn't a city left in the United

States that hasn't been affected by the opioid epidemic, and here was no exception. There were socio-economic considerations, complicated tribal matters and cultural clashes. A clear disconnect between the city, county, state, tribal and federal laws also did not help the problem. In regards to animal rights in particular, the laws change depending on where you're standing and who interprets them. It's a convoluted and contradictory mess. Through dozens of conversations I began to understand the Pandora's box he'd opened.

A permanent solution would have to be all-encompassing. It would require a functioning shelter equipped with volunteer staff and donation-based funding. There would need to be a massive, coordinated effort to spay and neuter not only the strays, but all of the existing household pets as well. For that to happen, free or low-cost vet services would have to materialize from somewhere and be available indefinitely.

Keith had far-reaching aspirations such as incorporating a community outreach division and adding an attached youth center. The shelter would be a place that had a few jobs to offer, hosted animal centered workshops, coordinated free spay and neuter clinics and maybe even somewhere kids that needed it, could get a warm meal. Keith knew from the very beginning that a solution for the animals would not be just about the animals.

The guy was clearly nuts in the head for even thinking he could do it all. But if he could actually pull it off—he would have the first successful and sustainable model of an animal rescue in North Dakota focused on serving a nearby First Nation. A model that perhaps could be scaled and taken to similar areas in need. I'd stumbled onto a problem that I couldn't turn away from and a person so motivated to fix it that I believed if anyone had a chance, he was the guy to do it.

Keith had to be particular about who he brought onto his team because so many of the animals rescued were on tribal land. The possibility of racial tension was high if the wrong people were coming around with ill intent. Getting the local community involved and gaining their trust was a priority. Anyone that was going to be a part of TMAR needed to be exemplars and advocates for the community. There was no room for prejudice, discrimination or intolerance. TMAR needed to prove to the community that every volunteer, no matter where they came from, was working for them, not against them. It sounds easy, but throwing different cultures together that don't know or understand each other well is bound to be fraught with misinterpretations.

At times, it all seemed so complicated. I thought we were just rescuing dogs, not solving world hunger. As it turns out, to really get to a long-term permanent solution, it was going to be a lot more complex than just rescuing dogs.

I considered whether Keith's mission and approach was the right fit for me. I also considered if I was the right fit for TMAR. There were herculean tasks that needed to be tackled and a real possibility that in the end we might have to walk away defeated, or die trying. I do like a good challenge but the one that lay ahead was almost paralyzing. I didn't know about a world divided by invisible political and tribal boarders. I didn't know the local ethos or traditions held dear that I might accidentally insult. I was a white girl, an outsider. I wanted to help but would have to prove myself competent enough to build bridges, not tear them down.

Admittedly, I knew nothing of the local history, but there was one thing I was sure of. Whatever I said or did, no matter if it was right or wrong, I cared about the welfare of the animals and the people. Whatever came out of me would only be intended to help, not harm.

I sent Keith a message one night, telling him that I was on board with everything in his vision and that I wouldn't quit. I promised to help and not give up, if he didn't either.

He responded back with something like this. "Animal people who actually get involved and stick, have a higher rate of crazy."

I responded with this. "So you think I'm crazy? Assuming I'm average crazy, then what are you?"

...

I needed to figure out where my skills were best suited to help him. I lived four hours away with a husband, kids, dog and work. I wouldn't be able to make the round trip with a frequency that would make an impact. Somehow, I would have to help from home.

My first task was to get the Amazon wish list updated—he needed supplies. His love-hate relationship with puppies was apparent from day one by the amount of bleach, puppy pads and paper towels that he requested. I was happy to help with the updates, but I knew that adding supplies to a list was not where I could be best utilized. I needed to do something that made more of a difference. I just didn't know what that was, but apparently, Keith did.

"You can write our stories," Keith said.

"Yes! Yes! I forgot! I'm a writer. I can write our stories."

A task for me that seems obvious now, but in my mind, at the time I thought rescue work was fostering, transporting, cleaning, and raising money. Who *writes* and saves dogs? The possibility had never occurred to me. Shouldn't I be out there moving animals and finding them homes?

I was writing other things completely unrelated to dog rescue at the time I met Keith. I didn't know if I was even capable of writing about what was happening with any level of competence. My boots were not on the ground picking up dogs or doing the real field work of rescue. I was mostly a behind-the-scenes volunteer. The plan was that Keith would let me know what was happening each day, then I would tell the stories of the animals that were rescued. My intention was to write and tell the rescue stories to raise awareness and maybe even a little money for a shelter. If just one person donated one dollar because of what I wrote, for me, that was considered a success.

I soon found out what Aliah had discovered months earlier. Keith was . . . picky. Very picky. For my first assignment he sent me a photo of some puppies he'd just picked up and a short sentence about where they had come from. They had been locked in a crate for months, given food and water, but likely had never been let out.

What kind of monster would do such a thing!? Hate and blame were my instant visceral reactions. I don't remember exactly what I wrote but it wasn't nice. Proud that I'd done those puppies justice and that their story might raise fifty dollars, I sent it to Keith for approval.

"That's not going to work. There is going to be a learning curve," he said. "I'll call you shortly."

I thought I'd passed the learning curve test, but nothing was as it seemed. I've helped build bridges but I've also inadvertently—and with great regret—knocked some down. Keith and I went through growing pains, and at times I thought of him as a ball-breaking New York editor who'd send back my good work with red marks just for fun. That wasn't the case. It was usually just because I didn't know all the facts. We communicated a lot through text message, and at first, much got missed or misinterpreted.

The puppies that had been locked in a crate were the result of mental illness, not intentional cruelty. Although evil humans exist, they were not a part of this story. There were only angels here. The moment one person became aware of what was happening they reached out and the puppies were rescued that same day.

When I found out the whole story, I deleted my initial writing and started over. I vowed to never make assumptions again. This was the first "story" I wrote for TMAR.

Some days it's one, others it's three. Today it was six.

Six puppies.

One small crate.

Three months.

The open sores on their feet are not as bad as we expected. After a bath, clean water and food fit for the little kings and queens they are, their paws and spirits will heal. Yesterday they lived in one small plastic crate, standing on top of each other, seeking reprieve from a four-inch floor of unimaginables.

Were they loved?

Yes.

But love wasn't what they needed.

Today they are roaming free and their bellies are full. They are biting and pouncing and chewing like normal baby fur monsters do. Let them chew the blankets, carpets, the couch, their bowls. They've earned it. They are survivors.

Six babies rescued today. #CratePuppies

Tomorrow there will be more, we will save them too.

It took me a ridiculous, God-awful amount of time to knock out those first three hundred words and they weren't even great.

Each week after that, I wrote three or four stories of the rescues Keith was doing. It was a fraction of how many dogs he was moving along.

Eventually my hard line editor fired himself, trusted me and let me fly without checking in for every word I posted. And fly I did, hurling us into the clouds, then plunging us right back down into the ground in an explosion that moved us forward yet set us back. Way back.

Fozzy's Story

For all the chain dogs who now get to run free and
for those we have yet to rescue, we won't stop fighting for you.

Fozzy lived his life tied to a tree behind a trailer. He had been there for seven years. A pile of trash to look at on one side, a heap of tires on the other and a small wooden doghouse nearby.

I was dispatched there on a call about an unresponsive individual. When I saw Fozzy it was like his five-foot chain was electrified, he was so excited to have some kind of contact. He choked himself against his collar so hard I thought he'd pass out.

I went in, made sure the guy was stable, and when the ambulance came I went out back to see Fozzy. I called him that because he reminded me of The Muppets. I had no option other than embrace the stink. I gave him a big hug and he hugged, licked, and rubbed right back. I kept Lysol in my trunk for getting the dead people smell off. I used some of that after Fozzy, then went back to my shift.

Every once in awhile, if nobody was home at the trailer, I would stop by, give him a treat and say hi. This went on years. I thought about him a lot, but there was nothing I could do. Then there was one too many unresponsive calls and Fozzy's owner didn't wake up.

That was the day I took him home.

I had shot some geese the evening before and I let him run loose as I started to clean the birds. He ran around a little then the wind kicked up and as I plucked, and the feathers flew across the yard. As I watched him run around in the feathers, I realized I was witnessing pure joy. I ran in and got my wife so she could see. We stood there choked up watching this chain dog run and leap and grab feathers out of the air. I have never seen pure joy like that in my life. I will never forget it.

CHAPTER TWELVE

Angels Fly

The ladies of Turtle Mountain Animal Rescue
Take over Half Brothers Brewing as your bartenders
December 9th for the UND vs St. Cloud Hockey Game
www.turtlemountainanimalrescue.org

HALF BROTHERS
BREWING COMPANY

(C.J., Jennie,Trista,Aliah)

I went on to help with future surrender events, shot clinics and a very small number of boots-on-the-ground rescue trips. For me, the real work came from the writing nook in my bedroom.

Each night after my kids were sleeping, I did exactly what I wanted to be doing—writing, rescuing dogs and drinking wine. It was perfect. Until it wasn't. Like all work-type situations, some co-workers you love, some you don't and the boss . . . well everyone complains about the boss from time to time. I, in particular had some beef with the boss when he suggested this.

> There are these two girls in Grand Forks and one in Canada that help with fundraising. I'm going to give you their numbers. I'd like you to connect with them.

I threw my phone down, rolled my eyes and let out a sigh. All I really wanted was to write and rescue dogs, by myself, without having to play nice in the sandbox with other women who could be crazier than me. But since he was asking, I had to say yes.

What I didn't say was that I hate fundraising. I was the worst kid in the class for going door-to-door and asking people to buy Christmas popcorn. I was the kid who sold just enough junk to my mom, dad and their co-workers to earn a blueberry-scented pencil. The last thing I wanted to do was call up three strange women and ask if I could be on their team because the boss told me to. But for Keith and for the dogs, I'd have to eat my feelings. So I did the only thing I could do, I called them.

What happened next was nothing short of miraculous. To my surprise and amazement on my first phone call with Jennie, Aliah and Trista, there was no talk of big galas and glitter balls and I sure wasn't going to throw any of that out there. I remained quiet at the mention of a silent auction, but other than that, the conversation didn't go nearly as bad as I thought it would. It went quite well actually. They were sort of . . . nice, smart, normal, and seemed every bit as motivated as I was to help Keith. We shared a common goal and similar level of crazy that kept us on the same page.

In the months that followed, each of us pulled our own weight. More than anything, we wanted to see Keith succeed in building that shelter. The goal was to raise ninety thousand dollars. We tried everything we could think of to raise the money. Some events went good—5k Run for Rescues, Pucks for Paws—and some went bad—Fifty Shades of Rescue, a giveaway on my author page, which although I should deny it, was my terrible idea.

We girls understood two things that motivated us to push through each day no matter how insurmountable our goal seemed.

1. We needed to show Keith that we could raise enough money to build a shelter. If we did that, he would stick around long enough for us to really solve this problem. We would have to do it before he burned out and threw in the towel. Which we felt was an imminent threat. Keith quitting due to burnout seemed to be a topic of conversation nearly every week. He dropped hints that he was drowning under the immense responsibility. But if he left, there was no one who would take over; certainly none of us with kids and jobs who live hours away from ground zero. We could support from afar, but if he wasn't there to pick them up and hold them until we could move them through the chain, it was over for TMAR.

2. There were dogs that were suffering. By the hundreds. Thousands over time and it had been going on for decades. None of us could sleep at night knowing that we were doing nothing about it and it was so close to us. We felt it in our bones to push forward. We had to raise enough money for a shelter before more animals died.

From selling stockpiles of hoodies, T-shirts and hats, monthly recurring donations and a handful of small fundraising events, each of us contributed to raising money. Now, at least, there was enough money to take care of the basic monthly expenses. We were finally able to cover basic supplies and food for the animals in Keith's garage so he didn't have to keep using his own money. That was a huge win for us and I really felt like we were making a difference in the lives of

Keith, the locals and certainly the animals.

Our goal was to continue to cover all monthly expenses and, on the side, save ninety thousand dollars. That would be enough to build a shelter. We didn't know how, or if it was even possible to raise that kind of money, but we committed and began to move heaven and earth to make it happen. Then somehow, Keith and the Angels began to soar.

I remember someone laughing at Keith, "You will NEVER raise that kind of money."

Keith straight up told the guy, "You don't know the Angels."

I got smarter and strategic about what I was writing and posting for TMAR. I found my groove and the rescue stories were starting to take off. Keith was taking better photos and began to do some live videos showing what he was doing up there. That caught attention. He was the heart and hero of the rescue and people were beginning to notice and tune in for more.

People began to talk about TMAR. A woman on a radio station four hours away said that if she got a dog she'd want a TMAR dog. Newspapers across the state inquired about what we were doing and published small stories here and there. I wrote an article about the rescue for a local magazine and we held fundraising events across the state. Steadily, we watched the TMAR bank account grow from ten to thirteen, then sixteen, and twenty thousand dollars. We absolutely couldn't believe it was happening! I remember looking at the GoFundMe account and watching it grow each week. I told my husband, I think we've doubled the donations in six months! Our efforts were working. Our once far off dream of building a shelter now felt like a real possibility.

We saved every dollar for that shelter. We asked for donations of bleach and dog food and supplies so we didn't have to use any savings. We were beyond grateful when people from around the country responded to our requests and started sending what we needed. Every bag of dog bones, donated leashes and every dollar mattered to us. We felt an extreme amount of gratitude for what was happening.

With increased followers and people invested in our cause came increased requests to help more animals, not to mention a surge of messages and emails that would all have to be answered. We didn't have the capacity to do all the things that were being asked of us.

Someone needed to manage the Amazon wish list. Someone needed to contact suppliers and ask for dog food donations. Someone needed to get the proper vaccinations for intake, pick up donations dropped off around ND, and keep track of and pay the vet bills. Who would keep receipts and do taxes? Someone needed to track the number of animals coming in, coordinate foster care, recruit foster families, coordinate transports and recruit people to transport. One person needed to do rescue-to-rescue relations so we could actually move all the dogs Keith was taking in along the rescue chain.

We needed someone to work on lining up the next surrender event and working with the spay and neuter clinic that was coming to town. What if a foster gets bitten? Do we need insurance? How much? Who? Where? What kind of policy? We don't even have an actual building. What are we insuring? Do we even have money for that? What if we can't raise enough money to keep going? What time can everyone meet to discuss and vote? Sunday 9 p.m?

There is a word for an organization that grows too fast and we referenced it frequently behind the scenes. We were a shit show. In many ways, we were a complete and total shit show. Even so, we were saving more lives than any other organization in the state or perhaps even in the upper U.S. We didn't know of another rescue that was moving seventy or more animals each month which further solidified just how crazy we all were for actually pulling it off.

With that kind of volume, we did good, we did bad, and we made mistakes. We got up, we fell down. We threw in the towel, then picked it back up. We laughed, cried and argued. We didn't talk to one another all day, then talked late into the night.

Thousands of lives would be saved if we succeeded in establishing a successful and sustainable model of rescue. If we burned out and failed, thousands more would die. The amount of responsibility on Keith's plate was unfathomable. After a year of nonstop growth, it seemed like he hadn't stopped to sleep once. Not that he didn't want to, he did, there was too much on the line and too many lives that would die if any of us stopped to take a breath or a nap.

We were growing faster than our four-kennel garage rescue could handle. It was more than Keith should, or could manage without losing a piece of his sanity each day. Eventually, it was also more than his marriage could take.

The problem is that it never ends. Rescue never stops. Just when you think you have a handle on it, the floodgates open up. The dogs and puppies never stop! Why? Why am I doing this?

Yes, I want to quit. I want to be responsible for me. I want my worry to be setting my alarm, getting dressed and going to work, then coming home doing something simple and going to bed.

I don't want to worry about fixing laws and regulations, trying to find out intra-jurisdictional land lease complications, finding a transport van that won't start on fire and has A/C for the dogs and windows that open in the back.

I don't want to worry about having a garage full of dogs, fosters that are all full, shelters at capacity, and more calls coming in. I don't want to play God.

Some days when you fall you just want to stay down and crawl off the road and sneak back into being normal. You want to be able to walk past a stray dog and turn your head and think, *someone else will do something*. What if you are that someone else? You have to keep doing what you do.

Everything, everywhere all the time is full. Fosters, shelters, rescues all at capacity and the critics that do nothing to save anything are unrelenting. It's bad enough dealing with the neglecters, abusers, and inept public officials.

"This stray dog wandered into my yard and I don't want it here, I need you to come get it."

"I'm sorry but I'm full right now, I have no place to put it."

"What the hell kind of rescue is this that you don't take dogs? Smh."

"I'm sorry, the rescue is my house garage, I just don't have anymore room and all our fosters are full."

"You guys are a fraud, you're just trying to make money, I'm going to tell everyone about how you don't really rescue dogs."

"Go fuck yourself," is what I want to say. I want to tell him, why don't you start your own rescue? Why don't you give up all your free time, and sleep and friends and relationships? Why don't you deal with the pain of seeing animals suffering, doing what you can and knowing it's not enough?

But I don't say that. I try and be nice. Let the asshole be an asshole because public opinion matters.

Because that's where donations come from. And without donations the thousands in gas and vet bills every month would break anyone but a millionaire.

You think about the 1992 transport van with 220,000 miles on it that two of the doors don't open, most of the windows don't work, and the engine fire that started and put itself out on the last transport. You think of sleeping on a pile of dog blankets on the van because you don't want to spend the money on a hotel after driving for twenty hours straight so you can make it home. It's all going for the greater good so like everything else, you swallow it. You swallow it and move forward because if you don't, they die.

You carry that weight and you let it push you through when you think about quitting. Then you YouTube a motivational video to get you out of bed and start Groundhog Day all over again. The day of the week doesn't matter because with a seven-day schedule, Monday is no different than Friday. The pee and poop and blood and tears will still be the same.

The problem with burnout is that you can't even run and hide from it. It's constant and I wake up and fight through it because there are dogs that need to be socialized and fed and cleaned up after even though on a bad day all you want to do is stay in bed, hide under the covers and make a little air hole to breathe out of.

You're in a state where you're nine hundred miles away from any family, you don't have time to spend with the friends you do have, so it's that awkward, "we have not talked in six months, but let's suddenly hang out."

Rescue isn't even a marathon. A marathon ends. Rescue is a never-ending march where everything in your path tries to stop or deter you, or slow you down. It's like trying to do a marathon except instead of people handing you water, they are throwing oil and thumbtacks on your path, lighting fireworks on the road, and telling you that you need to run faster or slower or backwards because whatever you're doing, it's not right or not good enough. But my reply is simple, "fuck off and get out of my way." If the path isn't clear, then I'll clear it because I am on an unstoppable mission to save lives and ease suffering.

Keith took it upon himself to be responsible for everything. As money came in, our rescue grew into a business and Keith became the business owner. He picked up the slack around every corner so what he said next registered as quite odd. Keith said he wasn't going to be able to answer his phone for a while. That we needed to take over all rescue business because he would have to keep his head up and watch his back.

But watch his back? For what? This is North Dakota, not Chicago. What he needed to watch his back for, we all wondered. It wasn't long before we realized what was up. There were some bad dudes in the area and a local dog wandered home with a human skull.

Imagine your beloved companion going out to go potty, then trotting back with a human skull in its mouth. He sets the bone he's unearthed on the deck and at first you think it's leftover Halloween decor from the fake graveyard in the woods, then you realize it's not.

It was a tall-tale, a crime scene straight out of the show *Forensic Files* and I didn't believe it at first. I'd heard plenty of small town rumors and lies to know that I must question everything—especially a fantastic fable such as this. I called

Keith to get the insider scoop on what became known to us as the Skull Dog. In true no BS fashion with no inflection in his voice, Keith laid it out for me.

> Drugs were being brought up from Detroit. Someone killed a guy in the woods, coyotes and dogs ate most of the body. Then some lady's dog brought home the skull. Police searched the area and found some other bones, the FBI took over I think.

Well folks, there you have it. Drugs, skulls, gangs, dogs, man-eating coyotes—all the makings for a Netflix original movie. I wasn't able to find out who the soul was that had been murdered in the woods or if anyone was ever charged. The Skull Dog went on with his life and found other less dramatic bones to chew on.

...

We went back to the business of rescue not knowing that we'd just gone through the storm before the calm. The whole world came to a halt. Everything seemed to just sway in silence, move in slow motion. We were left wondering if what happened next was the end of TMAR and the end of Keith.

Shots fired.

Officer down.

The original news article with video of The Skull Dog can be found here. https://www.valleynewslive.com/content/news/Dog-digs-up-human-skull-in-Rolette-County--421796273.html

999.1000.1001.1002.1003.1004.1005.1006.1007
.1008.1009.1010.1011.1012.1013.1014.1015.10
16.1017.1018.1019.1020.1021.1022.1023.1024.
1025.1026.1027.1028.1029.1030.1031.1032.103
3.1034.1035.1036.1037.1038.1039.1040.1041.1
042.1043.1044.1045.1046.1047.1048.1049.1050
.1051.1052.1053.1054.1055.1056.1057.1058.10
59.1060...
....
....
....
....
....
....
....
....
....
....
....
....
....
....
....
....
....1657.

CHAPTER THIRTEEN

Shots Fired

I had worked a long day on January 18. I got home at six and I was going off duty. I was waiting for radio traffic to take a break so I could call 10-7.

I called in and was getting my stuff out of the car as the radio was still going. I heard a call about a possible stolen vehicle headed to our county. The thing is, most stolen vehicles in every direction around us are typically coming to our county, so it was nothing new. If we found the vehicle, then it would just be another one to add to the thirty plus pursuits we have every year.

I thought about picking up the radio, but I was tired, there wasn't any imminent danger, so I shut it off. A lot of days I left my portable radio on in case something big happened, but that night I didn't for no reason other than I needed to deal with the dogs.

Maybe forty-five minutes later I got a message from a fellow deputy to call him right now. I did, and I knew something was wrong.

"What's up?"

"Colt got shot in the face. It's bad," he said.

"Is he going to be ok?"

"No. He's dead."

Deputy Colt Allery made the ultimate sacrifice while selflessly defending his community. He left behind his fiancé and five children. Deputy Allery, twenty-nine, and three other officers exchanged gunfire with the suspect following a vehicle chase. Colt was struck first in the cheek then a second and fatal shot went through his shoulder and traveled through his torso. The other officers on the scene all fired multiple shots at the suspect, killing him.

I don't remember what I said next, but I raced to get my uniform on and my wife asked what happened. I never thought about how hard on her that must have been. All we knew was Colt was gone and I was flying out the door.

When I got there, I did the same thing every cop did that night. Rush up to the scene even though there is nothing you can do. All you can do is stand there and look at your brother's body lying on the icy road and think about how you let him down. I let him down because I didn't ask about the truck that might have been headed our way. I didn't turn on my portable radio and listen to it, just in case. I could have got there in time. I could have taken a shot that could have stopped it.

When you're a cop, you rely on your fellow officers as your lifeline. The man or woman standing next to you is fully prepared to lay their life on the line for you just like you are for them. When a brother falls and you're not there to have their back, you fail them. It doesn't matter that you were off duty or on another call, you still failed them. You should have been there. I could have done a lot of things in my mind. Only time gave me perspective and understanding.

That was the first time I learned about a spirit fire. Where a fire keeper tends to the fire for several days, never letting it go out. We were invited to a service at the place where Colt had been killed. The leader of the service went to the exact spot where Colt's body was found. He lit sage, sweet grass and cedar. He said a prayer and explained there was so much pain at this place that Colt kept going between that spot and his spirit fire. He couldn't finish his journey until we let go.

He sang a warrior's song and a healing song. I never believed in organized religion, but for me this made sense. Not just because of the overwhelming trauma and grief, but because it felt real, it fit where no other religion had.

We gave offerings of tobacco and kept some with us. We left that place and left the bad with it.

The day of the funeral was rough. I'd gone through funerals for my family and even though Colt and I didn't hang out, it was just as bad because of the guilt that you didn't do enough. I saw the loss and pain of the community and felt the rage of injustice.

I think it was the morning of, when we were all contacted and told we were going to do end of watch—last call for him. One of our dispatchers was Amber, I don't know how she did it without breaking down, but she did. Each officer is called out on the radio by number, asked their status, and we reply 10-2, which means I'm good. When it got to Colt and there was no answer, it was like a sword driven through your gut.

At the end, when you hear "Deputy Colt Allery end of watch on January 18, 2017, we have the watch from here," you cry.

I sat in my squad car in tears.

Deputy Allery had only been with the sheriff's department for three months but previously worked for the city of Rolette Police Department and the Turtle Mountain Tribal Police Department. His death prompted thousands of law enforcement officers from across the country to drive to Belcourt for his funeral.

Keith was crushed. His wife sent a message to the team generally saying that Keith was going to be unavailable for a while. We were afraid *a while* could be forever.

We gave him space. It was unspoken, but there was an uncertainty among us. We knew it was rough being an officer up there. Really rough. Keith had told us stories about not having enough equipment to do his job properly and how his radio continually broke down, leaving him alone in situations he shouldn't have been alone in. How much more could he take of this place where the earth seemed to open and swallow him whole?

He mentioned buying land and a house in Louisiana. He told me how I would love New Orleans and that we could visit them there. He talked about the time he spent down south, fishing, shrimping, and stirring a big pot with a wooden spoon he used to cook a Cajun feast for his friends. When he spoke about that life Keith sounded like a different person, a whole person, a person not on the brink of burnout each day.

I thought TMAR was over. That Colt's death was going to be the death of Keith and the rescue. In my mind, I saw Keith packing up and leaving a forsaken place that had only brought him a life of turmoil since the moment he arrived. Little did I know that his heartbreak and tumultuous times were far from over.

In the weeks that followed Colt's murder, the airwaves between the team and Keith were silent. We suspected he was rescuing dogs on his own one or two, here and there. Messages came in and then disappeared, and he was not a guy to just delete a message about a dog in need. He needed to be solo for a while and we all understood that without judgment.

Five weeks after Colt was killed, two shots rang out again against a man in blue.

This time it was Keith.

CHAPTER FOURTEEN

Officer Down

Excerpts of the official police report written by Keith about this incident are denoted by different formatting throughout this chapter. Minor details like street names, addresses and directional cues have been taken out in an effort to make it easier to follow. In no way does this change the veracity of this account.

Keith was on patrol in Dunseith, North Dakota, when he pulled over a vehicle in what was supposed to be a routine traffic stop. As he approached the truck, the driver sped away. Keith followed him through town at speeds of fifty miles per hour. The driver swerved as he threw bottles of alcohol out of his window and back toward Keith's patrol car. Keith followed the truck to a remote, low-maintenance road until the vehicle got stuck in deep snow and stalled.

There were no houses, streetlights, traffic, or people in the area. The nearest house was a half mile away. The area was heavily wooded. I stopped my patrol vehicle, radioed in that I was in a foot pursuit, expecting the subject to get out of the vehicle and run.

I exited my patrol vehicle, drew my sidearm, turned the attached gun light on, and approached the vehicle. The driver was putting the truck in forward and reverse trying to get it unstuck. I called on the radio that the driver was still in the car, but got no response. Our portable radios usually do not work. I ordered the driver to stop and put his hands in the air. He took his right hand off the wheel and began reaching around the passenger seat area and dashboard of the truck.

I yelled several times for him to show me his hands. He continued to reach around in the vehicle. I radioed dispatch for 78 (assistance) but got no response. I again yelled at the driver to show me his hands and get out of the vehicle. The driver put one hand on the wheel and the other on the shifter. He continued to try and rock the truck out of the snow by putting it in forward and reverse.

I tried to open the door but it was locked. I told the driver to unlock the door and again ordered him out of the car. He did not comply. I kept my sidearm in my right hand covering the driver and with my left hand used my flashlight to break the driver's side window. It only took one strike to break the window, and the glass collapsed straight downward. The driver again started to reach around in the vehicle towards the passenger floor and seat.

Keith believed that the driver was under the influence of amphetamines. He put his flashlight away and used both hands on his gun to cover him while repeating verbal commands. Then Keith recognized the driver as a man he'd previously arrested for aggravated assault with a weapon and resisting arrest. The man had spent several months in jail during which time they got to know each other.

I said "Mike, stop it, you're under arrest, just get out of the car."

Mike briefly looked at me and said, "Fuck Keith, just let me go, please let me go Keith."

I again thought he was under the influence of methamphetamine, his eyes were glazed over and he was sweating and looking around quickly in all directions. He began yelling in a panicked tone about the cartel saying that they would kill him if he went back to jail.

I told him he was under arrest, and that if he did not get out of the vehicle I was going to spray him with pepper spray. He continued trying to move the truck. I gave him one final warning. He did not comply. I used one short burst of pepper spray into his eye and nose region. He yelled and briefly put his hands to his face, but then his hands went back towards the passenger seat trying to find something.

He was violently rocking back and forth and I yelled, "Show me your hands Mike! Show me your hands!"

Mike did not comply. I then gave him a longer stream of pepper spray directly into his eyes, nose and mouth. The spray had an effect but did not stop him. I told him to get out of the truck and put his hands in the air and I would clean his face off and get him some water. He ignored me and then started reaching frantically on the dashboard of the truck with both hands as if he was trying to find something.

I then shot a continual stream of pepper spray in his face, yelling the whole time to put his hands in the air and get out of the truck. At this point I did not realize that Mike had a loaded semi-automatic pistol on the dashboard in the area he was reaching. Mike started to reach towards the dash again and I gave him one final long continuous burst of pepper spray, emptying the can.

While Mike was somewhat incapacitated, Keith used the opportunity to reach into the truck, remove the keys and throw them away from the vehicle. He radioed dispatch that pepper spray had been used but again, got no response. It was then Keith knew the radio was not going to work. He seized the opportunity to put one handcuff around Mike while his hand was on the steering wheel. Keith jerked his arm out of the window, holstered his gun and told Mike that it was over, that he was going to jail. Keith had to let go of the cuff to get Mike's arm out of the window.

As he cleared the door, I positioned myself to take him down in case he didn't comply. I had my hand on the cuff on his wrist, but he twisted violently and hit me over my left eye. I saw the punch coming at the last second and lowered my forehead so I wouldn't take it in the eye. The blow landed just above my left eye. I saw stars and lost my balance, taking a step or two backwards.

Mike must have been walking at me as he was right in front of me, then he threw another punch. The punch landed somewhere on my head, he tackled me, driving me into the ground. When we hit the frozen ground, all of his weight was driving into my ribs. I felt a sharp pain and felt the wind get knocked out of me. I couldn't breathe.

As I tried to get up he started hitting me in the head from behind. I am unsure of how many strikes were thrown. I believe I was on my hands and knees at this point. I tried to turn but his weight was against me with his legs on either side of my body.

Then he landed one direct shot to my right temple. I was facing the ground and he was straddling me when the strike landed to my right temple, I knew he had a weapon. I had a dense stocking cap on, but through the cap I could feel that I had been hit with something hard and narrow. I had a previous assault case with Mike where the victim stated Mike had assaulted him with brass knuckles.

As soon as the strike landed I was dazed and saw stars. I have been knocked out before and knew that if I was unable to better my position and take a few more strikes, I would lose consciousness. I was in fear for my life at that point because Mike had purposely ambushed me. I thought he was high on methamphetamine, I could not communicate on my portable, I had no idea how far out backup was, there were no people, cars, or houses in the area, and I thought I might lose consciousness. My head was fuzzy, but I do remember thinking that if he did knock me out, he would take my gun and shoot me.

I reached for my weapon, drew it and yelled, "Mike, get the fuck off me or I'm going to shoot you."

As I brought the pistol up to try and shoot over my shoulder, Mike grabbed the barrel and yelled, "Don't shoot me Keith, don't shoot me."

I then told him "Get off me then Mike."

He again yelled "Don't shoot me Keith."

I again told him "I won't shoot you, but you have get the fuck off me."

Mike continued to try and get control of the gun. I think he was crouched over me and I believe I was on my knees. I could feel his chest on my back. The gun was still pointed away from me and he was trying to wrap his hand around the grip of my gun. The gun went off during this part of the struggle. Mike had one hand over mine on the grip of the pistol and the other towards the muzzle. He tried to turn the barrel of the gun towards my head. We struggled to control where the barrel was pointed. Mike was in a better position than I was. He was bigger and stronger and was able to slowly twist the barrel of the gun towards my head.

He was able to bend my wrist and arm so the gun was going towards my face. At one point I remember the barrel being pointed up towards my shoulder and about two inches from being in line to shoot me in the head. I do remember feeling some part of Mike's hand against my finger where the trigger was.

I continued to fight for control of the gun, trying to get the barrel away from pointing at my head and him trying to turn it towards me. I managed to get the gun back onto the ground with the barrel pointing away from both of us. The gun went off a second time. One of us had our hands on the slide, and when it fired, it was unable to eject the round. The empty casing lodged in the barrel and the gun was then rendered unable to fire. I did not know the gun was disabled at this point.

Mike again got a better grip on the gun and tried to turn it towards me once more. As the barrel came towards me again I thought I might be able to get a shot on him so I ducked my head to the right, pulled the trigger, and nothing happened.

The gun then went back to the ground with both of our hands on it. Mike had both hands pinned on the gun holding it against the snow, and I had both hands on the gun doing the same.

I again told him, "I'm not going to shoot you Mike, but you need to stop."

Mike shifted his weight and briefly took his left hand off the gun. I looked over my shoulder when his left hand was off the gun, and delivered a hand strike behind me to his groin. He winced and pulled away for a second. I felt Mike's weight come off my back and I used this opportunity to stagger away from him and then turn towards where I thought he was, pointing my side arm in front of me.

As I got up to my feet I was dizzy and saw that he had already got up and started to jog away. I again told him to stop, but he kept walking away quickly down the trail. I radioed, "Shots fired" and dispatch was finally able to hear as I heard them repeat it on the radio. When I went back to the sheriff's office the next day and replayed the tape, the only radio traffic that came across on my portable from that night was "shots fired."

I followed about ten yards behind him. While I was covering him with my sidearm in my right hand, I drew my Taser with my left. I told him to stop or he would get tased. When I fired my Taser, Mike briefly screamed then twisted and grabbed the wires that connected the probes to the Taser and broke them. He continued to walk away. I holstered my Taser because it would have taken both hands to load a new cartridge and I did not want to take that chance, as it had not been effective the first time.

I followed about ten yards behind with my gun drawn on him. I continuously ordered Mike to stop and get on the ground. I did not know how much further he would try and go, and I still did not know if he had another weapon on him. I covered Mike with my firearm and got closer, then I delivered a kick to his left knee. He buckled slightly, but did not go down. I again delivered a kick to his leg in the same fashion and he yelled and buckled but did not go down. I then heard someone coming up from behind me, I turned and saw a tribal officer jogging towards me. When the tribal officer got next to me he had his

Taser out and pointed at Mike.

While processing the scene that night deputies found a gun on the dashboard of the truck, a pair of brass knuckles and a knife laying on top the snow. Keith was taken to the local hospital and treated for several large lacerations and broken ribs.

Local news reported that thirty-three-year-old Michael Marion, originally charged with the attempted murder of Keith, pleaded guilty to numerous felony charges, including aggravated assault, attempting to disarm an officer, and possession with intent to deliver methamphetamine. He was sentenced to more than six years in prison.

Just one year before Colt Allery was murdered, Jason Moser, a Fargo police officer, was also shot and killed in the line of duty. His death was still a fresh wound for the whole state. With Jason, Colt and Keith on my mind, the reality of what was at stake for these officers was clear and haunting. Keith narrowly escaped with his life but I couldn't help but feel that it was a real possibility something like this might happen again.

Pickle's Story

Pickles was days away from death. His story is one that illustrates the unconditional and unstoppable force Keith is when it comes to helping animals in need.

Keith was at home trying to heal from broken ribs and a bout of pneumonia he caught just out of the hospital. He was under doctor's orders not to lift anything—especially not a ninety-pound St. Bernard. But what do you do when a St. Bernard who is near starvation needs help and you're the go-to-rescue-guy? You re-break your ribs trying to help, that's what you do.

Pickles' fur was matted worse than any other dog we'd seen. He had softball-sized mats pinning his tail to his back legs, and trash, dirt, burs and sticks woven into his neglected coat.

Keith found him in the ditch where he was reportedly last seen. Pickles was extremely weak and had a difficult time walking through the deep snow. Keith punched holes in the snow with his boots as he walked toward him, his own body aching with each step. They were a closely matched pair.

Like all the dogs do, Pickles walked away from Keith. Then Keith walked closer. Their dance continued until the big boy was too tired to go on so he just lay down and surrendered. Keith slipped a lead around his neck but it was apparent that Pickles had never been on a lead before and he wasn't about to go anywhere.

Keith was forced to drag him a few feet then let him rest and then drag him again. Once they got to the truck, Pickles wanted nothing to do with that either. Keith had no choice but to wrangle him in any way he could. Pickles was about ninety pounds, which for his breed, was forty pounds underweight. When Keith picked him up, Keith felt his rib pop.

Keith sent the team a picture of the beast he'd rescued and broken his rib for. We couldn't believe he was out there picking up dogs after everything that had happened, yet, at the same time, we could.

I came across a picture of Pickles a few months later with his new family. The dead dog walking looked like he was born again. I wanted to see what his life was like today. His mom Lindsay, sent me updated photos and said nothing would make her happier than to share his story.

Georgie's Story

Wisconsin 2018 - Lindsay and Georgie

"For the first two months, Pickles, (now George or Georgie) hid or attempted to just stay in one room with his face hidden as much as possible. He made no eye contact and cowered if we raised a hand to pet him. He was curious about us, but very nervous and shut down.

He was extremely weak and skinny. He tested positive for Lyme Disease and the vet told us he needed to gain forty pounds to reach a healthy weight. He started Lyme treatment and pain meds right away. He is an expert at hiding pills in his mouth and spitting them out.

Over the summer he started to gain weight and confidence and had more energy to walk and explore the yard. He began to realize that our other dog, Louise (aka Weezy) was going to be his friend and ally. By Thanksgiving and Christmas he began roaming the house, choosing to be in the same room as the rest of us and making eye contact.

He sought out attention from the kids and he decided to share his very loud bark with the neighborhood when outside.

He still hid when guests visited. He also developed canine bloat which we caught early and he had emergency surgery for. Because he gained weight and was healthier, his recovery was quick and easy.

We have discovered that George has a heart marking on his rear that seems fitting, as he is such a sweet and gentle dog. He loves Weezy so much (they are named after the couple from the 80s TV show "The Jeffersons") and likes to initiate explorations outside with her by barking in her face. I'm not sure it's her favorite.

He is now at the ideal weight and very healthy. His back legs are a little sore, probably from Lyme but, as I noted, he spits out any pain meds or supplements we give him. Like most dogs of his breed, he can be stubborn and, due to his size, he often gets his way! He drools, and we spend a lot of time cleaning drool off the windows, walls, and furniture. I will send you a video of his "magic ears.". He can lift his ears when he is interested in something being said to him!"

You can watch the video of Georgie's "magic ears" here.
http://bit.ly/GeorgiesMagicEars

CHAPTER FIFTEEN

300 Dead Dogs

 In the dead of winter sometimes there is a string of beautiful days when the temperatures hit fifty to sixty degrees. The sun shines, snow on the road melts, and you can hear a constant dripping of water as the winter coat that covers the land slowly dissipates. It's a glimpse of what is coming around the corner when spring arrives. New life begins and old life is uncovered.

On a few of those nice days, Jennie drove out to the area and took some photos to document the yearly die-off. One of the factors in solving the overpopulation problem permanently would be ending the denial that an animal overpopulation problem exists—a denial that runs deep. Not all, but some folks, who are often the loudest, believe that the amount of animals dying is embellished or fabricated. This attitude of looking away, although not the majority, has sentenced thousands of dogs to death.

I pondered why such a harmful denial exists, and can only assume that without resources to help solve a problem of this magnitude, hopelessness has set in. Denial is the mind's way of protecting itself when a problem is too insurmountable to comprehend or it too difficult to admit is real. Over many decades, perhaps compassion has been suffocated by hopelessness.

After Jennie took photos and documented what was happening, I did what I said I would do, what my primary job with the rescue was, writing. So . . . I wrote about it. None of us expected the media storm and community backlash that would ensue from my three hundred-word post. The stress everyone, especially Keith, felt before was nothing in comparison to what came after I tapped that one little blue button that said publish.

300 Dead Dogs Frozen to the Ground.

He reminds me of a dog from my childhood, Snowy, and I am instantly brought to tears at the thought. This one, what was his life like? How old was he? Was he ever loved once, even for a day?

On an ignored square of land, thirty-one by thirty-one miles, tragedy is hidden until the snow melts. Today the snow is melting.

Zero dogs rescued.

Spring is upon us and so it begins again. Those left in the reproductive cycle will have puppies, lots of puppies. The solution?

Rescue. Surrender. Spay and neuter. Resources to do all of the above. Tomorrow we will keep on.

The photo of the white dog was heartbreaking. At first glance you don't know if the wolf dog is sleeping or dead. One of the criticisms of me posting it was, "Why would someone actually post a picture of a dead dog?" The answer is because it was the least disturbing of all the dead dog pictures she took that day, that's why. I didn't say that, of course, because it would have only incited more hate. The team had dealt with enough dead puppies and suffering dogs that the white dog in the photo wasn't shocking, it was the same tragedy we'd seen throughout the winter. The same tragedy that motivated us to keep pushing forward and put all the systems in place that were needed to fix this.

I suppose to some degree we have become desensitized to seeing the dead dogs, but I can only speak for myself when I say that I am not desensitized enough not to cry, or that every puppy that comes through the rescue and doesn't make it, doesn't affect me in some way. Just recently, I bawled my eyes out over Lambchop.* The hurt of losing the rescue dogs, watching Keith find dead puppies or seeing the abused ones is never any less painful. You just get used to it being around more frequently.

My post set us back with the locals in a bad way. The controversy over that photo and what I said went on for weeks. It brought attention and criticism to a town and a people who weren't asking for it, didn't deserve it, nor did they have the resources to fix what was broken. People from all over the country, hidden behind a computer, were quick to point fingers and spread hate without understanding the totality of the problem.

The media storm around that post created stress among the team. We argued about what to do next and perhaps the whole debacle created resentment from Keith for even posting it. In the months that followed, I was on a tight leash with what I could post, and understandably so. After everything that happened to Keith in the last three months, the fall-out he now had to deal with from an angry community put tremendous strain on him at the worst possible time. For what he had to deal with over those three hundred words, I am eternally sorry.

One positive thing the post did do was show us how much support we had for what we were doing. It circulated, brought in new followers, flooded us with words of encouragement, stories of corroboration and much needed donations. It also brought to light just how much denial and misinformation was out there.

I was shocked at all of the people who were angry that we had "fabricated" that 300 dogs died that winter. When the rest of North Dakota began to circulate the post, local news spun it and publicized it in papers all over the state. The headlines got the story *almost* right, bringing the accuracy of the claims into question.

300 dogs found dead and frozen to the ground in Turtle Mountain**, North Dakota

300 dogs discovered frozen to death at Turtle Mountain

One of the articles went so far at as to say, "The couple drove around an area of land covering thirty-one miles and found 300 dead dogs." Of course, this was not what happened, those statements were taken out of context.

Anger, racism, support and everything in between flooded in through our Facebook page at a break-neck pace. Keith was the only one who could really clean it up with the locals because most of the local anger was directed at him. He was the face of the rescue, the Dog Rescue Guy. He was TMAR. The rest of the team was completely unknown and worked behind the scenes. Everything that was said on behalf of TMAR looked as if it came directly from him leaving him to deal with all the criticism. He put out the following post to try and quell the dozens of angry messages that began to come in.

> Just want to do a clarification post for people. One of our volunteers from Grand Forks came up and I drove her around to show her the problem.
>
> Did we see dead dogs?
>
> Yes.
>
> Did we stop and count three hundred that day?
>
> No.
>
> Did three hundred dogs die this winter?
>
> Yes.

In a separate news article a week later, he explained further.

> I had several messages about stray mothers that had puppies under trailers in early December. The people that messaged did so because they cared. What I ended up with was thirty dead frozen puppies from various litters. Some were emaciated and a little older, and some were only a few days old. Mom must

have gone out looking for food and the puppies couldn't stay warm enough. That was on four trips from people that messaged. How many people didn't message? How many dogs died in garbage piles and abandoned homes or trailers?

Throughout that winter, TMAR was moving up to seventy animals. Every. Single. Month.

Each one of them went through Keith's garage then along the rescue chain. Had Keith not been there to pick those animals up, most would have perished. Three hundred dead dogs that winter, in all likelihood, was a conservative number.

As the comments came in, they could generally be classified into one of four categories:

1. The Eye Witnesses

"My family has been blessed with a sweet girl that was abandoned just outside of Turtle Mountain. This is an issue and no one should even think twice about the story being accurate or inaccurate."

"Spring was so difficult to bear when I lived there. I haven't lived there in many years and am sad that this is still happening."

"They are trying to solve a problem that has been going on for years."

"You may not want to see it, but it needs to be seen. The rescue needs the funds to stop this from happening and they need to reach a larger population. Don't shove the situation under the rug."

2. The Misinterpreting

"There are several communities in the area, but everyone assumes it is only happening within the boundaries of the reservation. I'm not saying there isn't a problem, however most towns have problems with strays. This is a wide-spread problem in North Dakota and isn't exclusive to the reservation."

"If this happens every year . . . why doesn't the local shelter ask for help and network with other ones?"

"TOTALLY disgusting! Yet people refuse to spay and neuter. People keep on breeding trying to pad their own pockets. Makes me sick to my stomach!"

3. The Solvers

"I think a group of people need to put down and bury these dogs. Better than three hundred frozen dogs along the highway every year."

"Much like the death camps of Germany, I would make the people responsible for this to actually do the dirty work, maybe then they would take better care of their pets."

4. The Non-Believers

"So is there any proof of this story's veracity, or we're just taking the word of people with a GoFundMe and one sad photo? Three hundred is . . . an astonishing number and I am fairly skeptical."

"This article is a fake. The 'reporter' who made this up should look up the definition of reporting."

Then there was this little helpful comment I don't even know how to classify.

"Seems there is a problem that a rescue and a GoFundMe account will not solve because there are too many now. The most compassionate gift I could give rather than five dollars would be a box of bullets."

Oh and lest I forget . . . let me share my top two personal favorites. Just for fun.

"And now they want money? For what? Where were they when these poor dogs froze to death??"

"You cannot be doing your job wholeheartedly if three hundred dogs are found frozen in five months!! I can see a few that got neglected or wandered off! Three hundred?! Come on! Do your job!!"

I questioned whether I should repost some of those hate comments here but I decided that including them gives a more accurate picture of what the team had to deal with.

There were enough words said out of anger, support, misinformation and truth to wrap twice around the globe. Proving that it does not matter what I write, or what we do, even when it's the truth, there is always going to be someone trying to cut us off at the knees.

In the first five months of 2017, Keith endured the loss of a fellow deputy, the attempted murder on his own life, broken ribs, pneumonia and a media attack, courtesy of yours truly. Amid all the turbulence, he somehow managed to pick up 352 dogs and twenty-two cats; about twenty animals each week. The average intake for TMAR's four-kennel garage was seventy animals a month. We didn't know it, but that number was about to climb to over ninety.

There was one more animal rescued during that time that didn't get tracked in the database. One starving, emaciated animal that would earn Keith multiple criminal charges including possession of a big game animal and . . . lying to law enforcement.

*Lambchop was only with us for one night. He crawled into a stroller in someone's yard, they called us and Keith went to get him. There was nothing anyone could have done. The team found some small shred of solace in the fact that Keith cared for him during his last hours and that Lambchop slept in a warm, soft bed perhaps for the first time on his last night.

**There isn't a city in North Dakota by the name of Turtle Mountain. Turtle Mountain is a geographical land mass that rises 600 to 800 feet above its surroundings. The hills around it cover about a thousand square miles, half in North Dakota, half in Manitoba, Canada.

Arya's Story

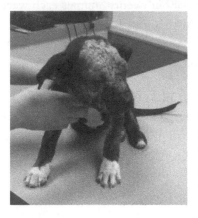

The dogs suffering from mange come with just skin and bones. Most of their fur is gone and they have sores and skin infections. They are constantly itching and in pain. They get treated as lepers. Nobody wants to touch them or be around them.

They are the lonely ones.

When I get them in I sit with them, pet and hug them and they just eat it up—finally someone wants to touch them and love them. Then I give them the first bath of their life. It's scary at first, but the warm water makes all the sores feel better.

I remember little Arya. Her poor head looked like a cauliflower. The swelling was so bad that she had trouble opening her eyes. Her whole head was hot, but just melted into my hand as she let out a little sigh of relief.

These are the ones that have kept me going—these moments. Where you get to ease the suffering of another living being, you get to take their pain away even if it's just for a little while.

The beard mange and body mange from the hugging sessions are always worth it—even at 3 a.m. when I'm trying to figure out how such an evil little bug came into existence.

I always hope for follow-up pictures of these ones. I don't get a lot, but sometimes when I do it's such a great feeling to see them doing so well.

Arya was found by Andy Laverdure, a judge and well-respected elder in the community. I reached out to Andy and asked him to tell me about the night he found her.

"When we found her it was dark. I was worried she would die. I called you guys right away. We get dogs dropped off near our house often. Must be our location—north of the dump ground. People can be so cruel. Abandoning dogs like that. We've taken in a few."

Andy and his family have acted as independent rescuers for many dogs. They have reached out to TMAR on many occasions when they have taken in dogs like Arya. All have moved safely and successfully along the rescue chain.

CHAPTER SIXTEEN

Saving Bambi . . . or Not

In North Dakota, "possession of a live wild animal is illegal. So, if you come across young animals while enjoying North Dakota, leave them where you find them."* That is exactly what the ND.gov website states.

Furthermore, the site recommends, "the best thing to do is leave it where you found it." Of course, in some cases that may be sound advice, but in others, it's downright ridiculous.

Wildlife rehabilitation (the act of taking in injured or sick animals, like starving fawns or baby birds that fall from a nest in your backyard and caring for them) is illegal in North Dakota. We are the ONLY state out of all fifty in the U.S. that does not have wildlife rehabilitation centers and makes it a crime for any citizen to help injured wildlife.** If I could insert the girl slapping her forehead emoji here, I would.

Hypothetically, let's say you ran an animal rescue operation out of your garage and had taken in thousands of sick, injured and unwanted animals over a few years. Then, let's say that on a sunny Sunday afternoon you were driving along when an emaciated baby fawn, not more than a few days old, stumbles into the intersection of a busy highway. You watch it almost get hit by a truck before it runs into a ditch only to get tangled in barbed wire. After you untangle the frightened baby, cut yourself and tear your clothes, you look around for its mother but for miles in every direction, there is nothing for mom or the baby fawn to survive on. Momma is not coming back. This baby has been on her own for days and will not survive.

Do you . . .

A. Tell Bambi you're sorry, but unfortunately she was born in North Dakota, the only state where it's illegal to help wildlife. The state has determined it's best if she just lies there and dies.

Or, do you. . .

B. Since you have some skills to help injured and sick animals, you pick her up, wrap her in a towel as she lies scared and trembling while you figure out how to feed her and give her a chance to survive.

B.

You choose B.

Congratulations, you've just landed yourself a misdemeanor! If you happen to be a sheriff's deputy and get slapped with a misdemeanor for taking in a dying baby fawn, instead of a pat on the back for being a compassionate human, you might lose your job.

At the time Keith took her in, neither he nor anyone else involved with the rescue knew it was illegal to try and help an injured wild animal. How would we have known? Before TMAR, every person on the team had little to no experience in the rescue world. We were thrown together by fate and bonded by a common goal. We were "The Breakfast Club" of dog rescue—each from a different background, each a little damaged in their own way.

I threw up a Facebook post about our newest edition to the rescue, broadcasting our nefarious activity far and wide.

> I was charged with possession of a big game animal and lying to law enforcement. They threatened to charge me with federal wildlife trafficking. I took the fawn home, got it some goat's milk, and after a day or two it turned around and got strong again. We had posted online that we were going to take it to a rehab center. One of the rescue haters turned me into ND Game and Fish who originally said if it *wasn't* healthy, they would put it down. They said if it *was* healthy, they would let it go in a field that had other deer. *Then* they said they would find a place at the zoo. A rescue friend said a lot of the deer at the zoo end up as food for other animals. I don't know if it's true or not, but I didn't want to take the chance. I never trusted what they were going to do as their stories kept changing.
>
> They, [Game and Fish] came to my house, I invited them to search the property and I showed them where I safely released the fawn. I was lectured about how me depriving the state of ND of a fawn

was a crime. I told them that sometimes in life you're faced with an easy choice or the right choice, and that I could live with the choice I made. Then I asked them to leave.

I was charged with possession of a big game animal. That charge was filed, but ultimately dropped as well as the charge of lying to law enforcement. The state attorney didn't want to waste any more taxpayer dollars to prosecute someone that rescued a fawn. The Fish and Game police put a lot of effort into the case and wasted a lot of money.

If you're wondering what ultimately became of the fawn, it survived. As for Keith's job, he wasn't fired, but he did resign shortly after. Not due to the Game and Fish debacle, but for reasons that had to do with safety. The basic things that deputies need to feel safe were not consistently supplied because of lazy attitudes and backwoods politics. It was common to have expired bulletproof vests, radios that didn't work properly, and be missing supplies that were necessary to do the job safely.

I had a foot pursuit with a guy who was on meth, bath salts, whiskey and Dilaudid. He was totally out of it, an obvious IV user and had blood all over him. I didn't find out until later that he had a terrible case of MRSA. The safest thing would have been to tase him, but I knew if I did that, it would be a month before I got a replacement Taser cartridge. So I had to take him down by hand. When I got back there were no drug test kits, no evidence tubes, no evidence tape or boxes.

> I just got tired of the mess. During an incident last fall there was a scuffle and I called thirteen times for dispatch with no response. I've never had a problem with the inherent risks of being a cop, but I did have a problem with the odds being unnecessarily stacked against me.

The residents of Rolette County poured their hearts out to Keith in the comments section of a Facebook post announcing that he'd resigned. It was clear—he was loved, admired and respected. For those that had gotten to know him they felt safe with him around. The residents lost a fair man and great protector, a sad day for an area that can be plagued with hardship and injustice. Just two months later, Belcourt lost another one of their own. Tragedy rocked the nation when headlines from North Dakota appeared around the globe.

It was one of the most brutal crimes of the century.

Consider adding your name on this petition encouraging lawmakers to make wildlife rehabilitation centers legal in North Dakota: https://www.change.org/p/allow-wildlife-rehabilitation-centers-in-north-dakota

*https://gf.nd.gov/wildlife/orphaned
**https://www.centerforwildlifeethics.org/killing-vs-saving-wildlife/

CHAPTER SEVENTEEN

Tragedy Rocks a Nation

On August 19, 2017 a pregnant Savanna LaFontaine-Greywind was reported missing from her Fargo home. Eight days later her body was found in the Red River a few miles from my own residence. She was no longer pregnant, and there was no baby found with her body. Savanna's newborn daughter had been discovered three days earlier alive and in good health. She was being cared for by the very people that murdered her mother and took her before she was born. The nation was shocked by her brutal death. Especially, the tribal nation. Savanna was born in Belcourt, she was a member of the Spirit Lake Tribe, her father is a Spirit Lake Indian and her mother is a member of the Turtle Mountain band of Chippewa.

The story of her violent death and the miraculous survival of the baby girl taken from her body spread around the globe. It was a tragedy that brought needed attention to the fact that specifically, on or off a reservation, Native American women are more at risk of many different kinds of violence. This problem must be rectified before the whole of any populace can be truly well. Where there is violence against women, there is violence against all other vulnerable groups, such as animals.

The interrelatedness of this crisis is real. Difficult work is ahead. A multi-faceted approach is the only way to a solution. Helping animals cannot only be about helping animals, it has to be about helping people too. No one is well until we are all well.

Michelle Obama is quoted saying, "The measure of any society is how it treats its women." North Dakota Senator Heidi Heitkamp must understand this. Since Savanna's death, she has introduced Savanna's Act. Caroline LaPorte, senior policy adviser on native affairs at the National Indigenous Women's Resource Center said, "The police response to cases of missing Native American women has been riddled with prejudice," and that "often, no report is taken at all. Savanna's Act focuses on this issue." LaPorte stated, "The bill's greatest accomplishment may be raising public awareness of this issue."

According to the Department of Justice, Native American women on some reservations are murdered at ten times the national average.

"Of over two thousand women surveyed, 84% of Native American and Alaskan Native women have experienced violence, 56% have experienced sexual violence, and of that second group, over 90% have experienced violence at the hands of a non-tribal member. Most women reported they were concerned for their safety and around half said they had experienced physical violence like pushing, shoving, or being beaten."**

I wanted to know firsthand how difficult it was as a Native woman growing up in the TMAR area. I sat down with a friend of mine who grew up on the Turtle Mountain First Nation in

Belcourt. I'd bumped into her a while back at a dog rescue fundraiser and I remembered her telling me she grew up there, and that her grandma took in stray puppies when she was a little girl. I sat down with Shelly over some craft beers and vegetarian pizza.

At first glance, she and I could be sisters. We share deep brown eyes, long dark hair, naturally tan skin and a stereotypical Fargo accent which includes vernacular like, *you betcha* and *don't cha know*. Shelly and I worked together fifteen years earlier serving bar food and drinks. I was eighteen and she was a few years older. At the time I didn't know where she grew up or anything about her. I just knew I liked her and that we worked well together. She was honest, straightforward and lifted other women up. Shelly is the same woman today.

"There were tons of strays," she said when I asked what the situation with dogs was like when she was growing up. "I stayed with my grandma on the weekends, she had a place in the country and stray pregnant mommas would wander in all the time. They'd give birth and then leave. I remember bottle-feeding the pups with a baby doll bottle. When they were old enough we would throw scraps out. The same scraps we threw out for the pigs." When I asked what they did with all the puppies she said they would give them away to family or friends. "But a lot of folks didn't have any money to take care of them. The cost of getting them fixed was so high and the nearest vet was more than an hour away. Some folks don't even have cars or enough money for gas even if they wanted to take care of them like they should."

I asked her what it was like growing up in small town North Dakota, on the reservation. "It was all about who you knew. All about politics," she said, shaking her head in apparent frustration. "I moved away two months after I graduated from high school and never went back. There was nothing for me there. The schools were great though. I still remember some of my teachers. They all genuinely had an interest in seeing you succeed." As we talked and drank our beers she expressed her irritation with small town gossip, the constant politics with a dash of corruption. I got the sense the problems there were not so different from any rural area with dwindling jobs, little for young adults to do, and increasing problems with addiction.

I asked Shelly to shed some light on what she felt was the general attitude toward dogs where she grew up. What she told me was difficult to hear. She said some people have become immune to seeing dogs suffer, but that is not reflective of everyone. "People shoot dogs there, they don't care whose dog it is. If it comes on your property, it gets shot. There was a lot of that. There was a lot of dogs that got hit by cars too, that was really sad. It was awful." I asked her about wintertime, about the dogs that die from exposure. If she had firsthand experience with that. "Oh yeah. Big time. Porch puppies froze all the time. If we found them, if we knew they were out there we'd bring them inside. But not everyone did. Lots of them froze." It seemed that the old mindset of "it's just a dog" was, and for some still is, deeply embedded today. "Taking care of the dogs was the least of anyone's worries."

Today, Shelly has three small dogs of her own. She showed me pictures of her fur babies and her human babies too. We compared notes about how good our kids have it and how they have no idea what it would be like to grow up in the circumstances she did.

I thanked her for her time and candid answers but left our dinner date feeling solemn. Maybe it was the drinks that got to me that night. Maybe it was just a bad day and I was in a mood. But the funk I came home with was one of hopelessness. I even argued with my husband, telling him I was giving up and that I couldn't watch it keep happening with no end in sight. It had been going on for so long, who was I to think change could happen within a population I knew little about nor had any influence?

Dogs, because people suck.

Strong Hearts Native Helpline 1-844-7NATIVE (1-844-762-8483) Their website states that a culturally-relevant, safe and confidential resource is available for Native American survivors of domestic violence and dating violence. The hotline is the first national crisis line dedicated to serving tribal communities affected by violence across the U.S.

*https://www.hcn.org/articles/tribal-affairs-why-native-american-women-still-have-the-highest-rates-of-rape-and-assault
**https://www.publicnewsservice.org/2017-12-26/human-rights-racial-justice/will-savannas-act-protect-native-american-women/a60750-1
***U.S. Department of Justice Office of Justice Programs National Institute of Justice RESEARCH REPORT NATIONAL INSTITUTE OF JUSTICEfile:///C:/Users/cenglish/AppData/Local/Microsoft/Windows/INetCache/IE/Z65UHD1F/249736.pdf
Violence Against American Indian and Alaska Native Women and Men 2010 Findings From the National Intimate Partner and Sexual Violence Survey By André B. Rosay, Ph.D.

Daisy's Story

"Hey guys, there's a stray boxer dog in the trees by my house with a broken leg. He can barely walk or run and it's in the same trees my husband just spotted a mountain lion, so it's not going to last long. Can you please come get him? He's nice and walked right up to my neighbor who was out there checking on cattle . . ."

"We're very sorry but due to a parvo outbreak we are closed for two weeks. If you can keep him safe, we'll get there as soon as we can. In the meantime, we can provide dog food if you need it."

We got there as soon as we could and he turned out to be a she—a sweet little thing named Daisy. The vet said he couldn't be sure, but most likely, she was hit by a car. One of her hind legs was completely crushed. Her entire hip joint had to be rebuilt. Committing to animals that need thousands of dollars in vet care is not a light decision. How many dogs can be saved with the thousands of dollars we spend to save one dog? But when we save one, we save it all the way.

The night Keith brought Daisy home she was emaciated, starving and broken. It was heartbreaking to see. Keith sent the team a picture of her snuggled under a blanket later that night after she had a warm dinner and as much comfort as he could give her. I recognized the blanket she was snuggled in, the ottoman she was lying on, and the television in the background. She was in Keith's living room, not in a garage kennel. I'd seen a handful of other dogs, the ones in the worst condition on that same ottoman, under that same blanket. For a few special ones, he lets them inside his home and into his heart a little more.

Daisy found her way to a foster family in Fargo who had a dog that looked nearly identical to her. The plan was to keep her until she was fully healed or at least until she could be moved to another rescue and put up for adoption.

That never happened.

During Daisy's difficult recovery, the foster family reached out to tell me the news. There was nothing else they could have done. It was inevitable given her condition and circumstances. She was never meant to go to another rescue.

Her home was with them.

1658.1659.1660.1661.1662.1663.1664.1665.1666.
1667.1668.1669.1670.1671.1672,1673.1674.1675.
1676.1677.1678.1679.1680.1681.1682.1683.1684.
1685.1686.1687.1688.1689.1690.1691.1692.1693.
1694.1695.1696...

....

....

....

....

....

....

....

....

....

....

....

....

....

....

....

....

....

2828.

CHAPTER EIGHTEEN

Madeline

Just as a snake sheds its
skin, we must shed our
past over and over again.
-Buddha

I reached out to Madeline, another young woman who grew up in the area near Shelly. I wanted to know what her experience was. Did she see frozen puppies or hundreds of strays too? Did she get the overwhelming sense that dogs are just dogs and that some people did what they could, but it was never enough? Or was she part of an awakening I so hoped had been happening all along?

Madeline shared with me her deeply personal experience about growing up in an area overpopulated with strays and how she came to be an independent rescuer. The story she told was tragic and inspirational—a tale that swung my emotions like a pendulum from one extreme to the other. Ultimately, she gave me back the hope I was looking for. The need to feel like all the hard work Keith and the team were doing would last a lifetime and beyond. She proved that it wasn't all just for nothing.

Her story is painful but it shaped the animal advocate that she is today. Madeline has saved hundreds more lives than she has taken. For that, I hope she can make peace with her past.

Madeline-2018

"At the age of five I learned how to shoot a gun, how to shoot dogs, and how to protect myself. When my father left he said it was my job to protect the house. He made sure I knew how to shoot the stray dogs that came into my yard in the stomach. That way they ran home to die and we wouldn't have a mess to clean up. I never understood exactly why. I just knew it was my job to shoot stray dogs.

By the time I was five years old there were a good ten dogs that I'd grown to love, that died. I was raised with the thought that they were there to live for a few days or a few years and then die. That was my experience, so it had to be true.

The first time I remember connecting with a dog on a spiritual level was when my dog became sick. He was a little brown mutt. He began foaming at the mouth and became very aggressive. He started to stalk me, my sister and my mama. I got a phone call from my dad who was out of town working. He said, "Madeline, it's time to shoot your dog. You have to." So I continued the business I did not understand. Why did I have to shoot my dog? I didn't know why. I just knew I had to. So like Daddy said, I shot him in the stomach. He went to his doghouse and I heard his cries. I went running over to him to try and save him but there was nothing I could do. Dad called me and I told him what I did. He said I needed to shoot him in the head. I had to walk up to him, I had to look him in the eyes, I had to see that pain, that hurt, that betrayal in his eyes and I had to aim my gun and shoot him.

From that moment on I cherished every animal's life.

My time shooting birds, playing with my BB gun or my .22 was over. I no longer could do that. I understood the quality of life that these animals have and the soul that I'm ripping out of them with just a bullet. From then on I had many dogs. Their average lifespan was two to three years so I never got to fully know any dog. I would get home from school, run off the school bus and into my house to feed my baby pups. When I wouldn't find them, my mom would tell me they got out and haven't returned. I walked miles and miles and miles, a child trying to find her pups. Sooner or later I would find them alongside the ditch, shot. They were always shot.

In some ways I grew up hating animals because they take your love and trust and then they die. Animals are the thing that I wanted in the deepest part of my heart, but my brain said they die, so don't connect with them.

When I was a teenager driving around town, I would see the dogcatcher throwing these bags in the river. As teenagers, we're going to want to look. And when we did we would find bags of puppies. It became our job to scan the riverbanks and watch for them, to make sure that no more puppies would drown.

The first moment I truly felt complete and total love, was at a time I did not believe in love for myself. I was in the addict. I was totally lost, submerged in my addiction. I prayed to God to give me a reason to live, to give me something to look forward to the next day. One day I got a message on

Facebook that said there were four-day-old puppies that were being given away for free because the mom had died. I replied and the next day I met this guy and he had three near lifeless things in a box.

I searched every friend's house I knew to find a bottle. I sold my personal stuff just to get milk for this little puppy. Watching her grow as I fed her, teaching her to go potty, from her I learned love. True love that people search years to find. I found hope, I found a reason, I found my best friend. I didn't know what I was doing, but I knew I had to keep her alive and in her survival I found my sobriety.

I have held her since she was five days old. I've lost her twice. It was a learning experience with bottle feeding and raising a tiny puppy that young. I have given her CPR, I wish everyone had that experience so they can see how human these little puppies are. To date she is my protector, she is my savior and she is still my best friend. Giving an animal a home, a safe place to be with love and food and affection is the lowest price any person can pay. I take comfort in being able to drop a bowl of food for someone's dogs. I don't care if I'm the weird chick. I also carry food for the little tiny humans who are hungry.

If a child cries out for help and none is given . . . a dog is just a dog. I know many people with this mind frame. My dogs are my children. I could never imagine hurting an animal again. They brought me life when I no longer wanted to live."

...

I asked Madeline if she felt like the general attitude among the local people had changed since TMAR began to rescue dogs.

"Ultimately, he's [Keith] viewed as a white dude taking dogs and turning a profit. I don't know how much of a heart-warming effect that has, but I think they see the change happening. Many people that are still here are in the mindset of our grandparents, that our culture was beaten out of us by white people. People are in the mindset that they are trapped here. I hear so many people talking about TMAR and the base of it is good, but that's in Dunseith. Belcourt, not so much. But before Keith, the big joke was you could go to the Turtle Mountains and can pick any breed you want off the road."

Remington's Story

He looked like a little, brown fox when he came in to the rescue near midnight. The scared dog held his head low and down to one side, he was in obvious physical and emotional pain. He'd been shot in the neck.

When a dog like Remington comes in, the whole team is on heightened alert. We all know that a gut-wrenching choice might have to be made—a choice no one wants to even think about having to make. Tension looms over every conversation. Each of us is silently wondering if we are going to have to discuss our options.

Are we going to have to put this dog down? How much pain is he in? Is it even fixable? How much will his vet care cost? Can we afford to find out?

What if we pay for all the diagnostic care and he has to be put down anyway? How much have we spent this month in vet bills already? How much more can we spend and still pay our expenses and save for a shelter?

There was no particular reason we chose to go through with getting Remington all the care he needed to survive including a complicated, risky surgery. We had compassion for Remington in the same way we had compassion for every other animal that came through. To us, he was no different, no more or less worth saving. Every life that came through deserved to not suffer and have a chance to thrive. But because there are so many, not only here but everywhere, there is just not enough resources for them all. Sometimes, hard choices must be made to save the most rather than the expensive few.

On the night the little, brown fox dog came in we didn't even discuss his plight. It was nearing midnight and the whole team was exhausted, especially Keith. We had the platform to try and raise enough money to save Remington, so we just did. There was no discussion. Each of us knew that every dollar we spent on anything other than saving for a shelter, or spay and neuter, was potentially condemning so many more to death over the years to come. Right or wrong, we just did the best we could do in each moment.

Remi now lives with a family in Wisconsin. Like Daisy and many other TMAR dogs, Remi was a foster fail—the term used when a foster family fails to help get them adopted and decides to keep them instead. Not a bad thing for the dog of course. Sometimes not a good thing for the rescue that loses a valuable foster family.

I reached out to Kayla, Remi's new mom to see how he is doing today. She said when Remi got to their home after surgery, he was in a neck brace and had significant nerve damage to the entire right side of his body. Kayla also said when he arrived he was very shut down, afraid of men, and didn't want to be petted, touched or brushed by anyone. He spent most of his time hiding behind the bathroom door.

Kayla and her family are now happy to report that his emotional scars have healed and he is a happy, friendly family dog. With the exception of his right front leg that buckles on him from time to time, he has healed physically as well.

I can't help but think back to the night Remi got to Keith's garage. If we functioned like so many rescues have to function—by policy and procedure alone with no wiggle room for gray decisions, Remi would have been put down. Do those rescues save more by euthanizing a few? Perhaps.

Critics are not welcome, they add to the emotional trauma the team already has to endure. When they do sneak in, they set everyone back and cause the pain from difficult decisions to linger. In rescue, there can be no judgment, no right or wrong. Dog rescue is an emotional roller coaster where people are trying their best to help fix impossible situations that require impossible decisions.

Check out the video of Keith and Remington just after he came in to the rescue. In this video, Keith mistakenly refers to Remi as a girl. He didn't know anything about the little, brown fox or the extent of his injuries. http://bit.ly/RemingtonsStory

CHAPTER NINTEEN

Turtle Mountain, Meet Harvey

So what do you do when you've left your job as a deputy and live in a county that has no other jobs to offer? You go to Texas and rescue animals— that's what you do.

Turtle Mountain Animal Rescue, a small but mighty force with a heart for animals everywhere was going on a rescue road trip.

In August 2017, Texas experienced record-breaking storms. Hurricane Harvey kicked off a historically destructive season in the south and throughout the Caribbean. Keith was heading right for it. There would be high water, extreme heat, and stranded and starving animals in need of someone who knows how to handle them. Keith was a perfect fit. His skills were uniquely suited for this type of rescue in the trenches.

I've had many conversations with Keith about the emotional and physical difficulties of rescue work. Like the times when he's there with the dogs in the end, and the insane amount of daily responsibility. It wasn't until he told me about Texas, that his voice broke and his emotions silenced the air between us.

When Harvey made landfall, the Angels were still in full force but there was now a handful of others helping behind the scenes. Every one of us wanted Keith to drive down and help with the animal rescue efforts. Whether it was helping families rescue stranded pets, working to get shelter dogs to higher ground or into shelters farther north, we knew he had to go as quickly as possible. If the horror stories of what happens to animals in shelters when natural disasters hit were true, Keith would need to do everything he could to save as many as possible.

We discussed if it was a good idea to send Keith to the opposite side of the country to rescue animals when there were still so many animals that needed help here. The answer we agreed on was this: what was happening in Texas was an extreme humanitarian crisis that could benefit from skilled hands on deck. If a tornado hit our area and displaced our animals and us, we would want people who knew what they were doing to help. Keith also needed some time away from the garage and for him, somehow extreme water animal rescue was a vacation.

The volunteers back home would help to cover what needed to be done and we were committed to helping raise enough money to cover his trip. The plan was set in motion.

Step 1. Keith needed to be self-sufficient with all the supplies necessary for a long trip south. Drinking water, food, gas, a canoe and as many kennels as he could fit in his truck. It was important to all of us that in the aftermath of a national disaster, he was not going to be an additional burden on already sparse resources. Keith took extra care to make sure he had everything he needed to live on loaded up in the back of his truck.

Step 2. Keith needed someone to ride shotgun. Someone willing to drive for days, sleep in a truck and tackle any possible situation that came up. Instead of finding someone we all knew, a friend maybe, or perhaps family—which would have been too predictable and boring—Keith found someone new. Chelsey,* a mom, wife, and volunteer with a big heart who was not afraid of dirty or hard situations. I reached out to Chelsea to tell me about her rescue trip with Keith.

"I was one of the fifty people that responded to stranger Keith's Facebook post. I never in a million years thought he'd pick me. On September 1, I met him at Walmart in Wahpeton. I have a friend who is a bureau of criminal investigation agent and I had him drop me off to ease the minds of the people that were begging me not to go. Luckily Keith and I hit it off immediately. He's not a radio guy, so we filled the hours with conversations about life, religion, food . . . anything and everything. Once we got there, if the water didn't stop you, the cops did. Keith still had his badge so he'd flash that and they'd let us through."

The first few days, Keith and Chelsea were trying to find their way around the mess that was Texas in the aftermath of Harvey. They found out firsthand how difficult it was to help in a crisis situation. There seemed to be more roadblocks than open doors wanting their help, but eventually they found their way to a place where they fit in perfectly in Bay City, Texas, alongside the crew at Shutt'er Down Ranch.

"Shutt'er Down Ranch was a rescue from Farmersville, Texas, that had set up a staging area. Rescue is organized chaos. I'm not kidding you. There were people, pigs, dogs, horses, even a rat. I ended up doing intake for any animal that came in the door. They'd come in waves. Sometimes two or three. Sometimes animal control would come back with thirty. I fell into this group perfectly. Everyone looked out for one another. Especially Rogue One, as we called him (John NeeSmith.) John is the epitome of everything you think of when you think of Texas. Tall, beard, gruff voice, always a stern look but kind eyes, and enjoys blasting his dixi horn. Keith and John hit it off immediately. Finally, this was the type of work we'd driven across the country to do."

Along with the crew at Shutt'er Down, Chelsea and Keith found themselves on a mission to rescue nearly a dozen horses that had been stranded in chest-high water for a week. A horse can lose twenty to forty pounds a day shivering in cold water, so everyone knew they wouldn't make it much longer if they didn't get there soon. Due to politics and power trips, the horses were in grave danger and efforts to get them out were thwarted at every turn.

In order for their rescue to happen, property lines would be crossed and permission needed to be granted, meter numbers required for transporting livestock needed to be obtained by the Sheriff—who apparently didn't have the authority to grant them in a state of emergency. To get anything done, people in power had to be contacted in offices that were underwater and out of operation. Keith recalls the team of rescuers being told they'd be arrested if they got the horses without the proper permissions. They called city council, animal control and everywhere else they could think of, but there was no answer. Under a declared state of emergency, no one was available to grant them permissions, anywhere.

People from multiple rescue organizations were involved along with the owner of the horses who was unable to get them out himself. Even though he needed assistance, permission would need to be granted by the county if anyone other than the owner was going to transport or rescue livestock—permission that could not be obtained in time.

> I said fuck this, we're going to make it happen, we're going tomorrow. I wasn't going to stand around any longer waiting on someone to do something. I talked to the owner of the horses over the phone. He was a real nice, country guy, real respectful but couldn't do anything himself to get them out. Sell me your horses for one dollar, I said to the owner. I'll get them off your property and then I'll sell them all back to you. It'll be a handshake agreement.

The deal would make Keith the rightful owner of the horses and enable him to rescue them without breaking the law. A staging area was set up with horse trailers and provisions for the team and the animals. They were finally able to start wading through the high water to get the horses out.

> There were two dead horses in the barn, and two dogs alive. Some of the horses came walking up toward us but the ones in the back just wouldn't come. John went back there but they just would not

go with him. One stepped on his foot twice. It turned
out that the reason they didn't want to go was
because there was an alligator in the water, a big
alligator. But John didn't care. He was eventually able
to lead them out.

The fearless crew navigated through chest-high water littered with debris, downed electric lines, and one displaced alligator before finally escorting the horses to dry land. The horses had been standing in water for more than a week, they were skin and bones and all were in critical condition. Keith recalls going in three times in total to get them all out.

For half a mile the highway was submerged as they pulled the rescued horses in the trailers toward safety. Keith flashed his badge at a checkpoint and police let them through with his newly purchased herd. Chelsey helped set up stations with hay and water, and the horses ate their first meal in weeks while the crew worked tirelessly picking fire ants out of their tails and tending to their rotting skin that had open wounds and cuts.

The horse girls (a rescue group from Florida helping
with the mission) were the best team you ever saw.
They were fighting to keep the horses alive, doing
anything they could. They took over their care,
worked on them for hours through the whole night
not knowing if they would make it.

The crew lost three horses by the next morning and more in the days that followed. It was an emotional time for everyone involved. It was tragic that the horses had to die because of what can only be considered a total failure by the animal control system during a time of crisis.

As much as sixty inches of rain fell in isolated spots over a five-day period. Hurricane Harvey will be remembered as the wettest tropical cyclone of all time, and one of the costliest hurricanes on record to ever strike the U.S.

> I'm forty-six and I've been through a lot of shit and that was the first time in my life I saw the good in humanity, the true good. The outpouring of support was amazing. Everyone came together, no race, no sex, no religion, no politics or any other divisions. It was just people helping people. No one had ever heard of the Turtle Mountains, but they were very glad the community had pitched in to send us down. I learned what Texas strong was and they learned what Turtle Mountain strong was.

So what do you do when you've just left your job as a deputy, go to rescue animals in Texas, and a hurricane again hits just a few states away?

You go to Florida and rescue animals—that's what you do.

*After hurricane Harvey, Chelsea Rongen now has three dogs, all rescues. One is from Texas, named Texas.

John NeeSmith and the guys at the Shutt'er Down Ranch can be found here: https://www.facebook.com/SDRanch/

The women from Forgotten Horses Rescue, Inc can be found here: https://www.facebook.com/Forgottenhorsesrescueinc/

Watch the live video of Keith in the flood waters here: http://bit.ly/HorseRescueInTexas

CHAPTER TWENTY

Turtle Mountain, Meet Irma

Sixteen days after Hurricane Harvey displaced an estimated thirteen million people in Texas, Hurricane Irma made landfall in Florida. With 130-mile an hour winds, Irma devastated much of the southern part of the state and the Caribbean.

There were ten hurricanes in total, six category three or higher, that would wrap up the 2017 storm season—a year of extreme weather activity well above the thirty-year average. According to an article in *National Geographic*, the damage from the 2017 hurricane season was the most expensive in U.S. history.* It's a good thing climate change is a hoax, or we'd all be in real trouble.

> Florida was a shit show. There was no formal anything. Everyone got turned away. There was no coordinated effort and the government was doing everything they could to keep rescuers out. Yet in the end, everyone came together and made it work. All the rescuers did amazing jobs saving lives. You realize how important pets are to people when faced with situations like this. They're not pets or animals, they're family.

Keith found a place for his skills in parts of Florida that needed him most. Much like his home base in North Dakota, Keith put himself to work in the most underserved neighborhoods that were the last to get help. This time, instead of rescuing dogs or horses, he stepped in for the feline kind, assisted disabled families, and fired up a chainsaw to do some much needed hard labor. Few other people would task themselves with clearing away fallen trees covered in fire ants in ninety-eight degrees and 100 percent humidity.

Keith came back with too many stories of precarious ladders, parasitic infections, and larger-than-life personalities to tell here. However, there was one woman in particular he talked about repeatedly. Her passion, her heart and her mission seemed to motivate him. Dori at For the Love O' Maxx in Bonita Springs is an independent rescuer, caring mostly for cats. What Dori is doing out of her home matters to so many animals and she is an example of someone who asks for no credit, gets no recognition or money for saving countless lives. Dori takes in the animals no one else wants.

Keith told me how much he wanted our team to support her small-time operation and I saw the parallel, why his heart bled for what she was doing. She was him when he first started. No money, no help; a nobody from nowhere who stepped up when no one else did, to save animals no one else wanted. Dori and Keith saved countless lives from the shadows.

Then Keith found a tribe of his own. Together they stepped into the light, broke the mold, challenged the system and changed status quo. They were fearless in a world where cowardice kills.

As stories of hurricane animal rescues were broadcast all over the U.S. in the wake of the 2017 disaster season, a heaviness plagued me and threatened my fearlessness. The scope of just how many animals needed rescuing everywhere—not just in my own state, but around the globe—was as unfathomable as it was tragic. Sometimes, only for a moment, other times for days, I was discouraged by the fact that if everywhere else in the world couldn't figure out how to solve these problems, who were we to think we could?

During times of high volume intake, it felt like we were getting nowhere, not even making a dent. How can we rescue seventy to one hundred dogs each month for years and still more keep coming in? We needed to put other measures in place to become more than just a pipeline. First, we had to establish an adoption division. That would save on transportation costs, put animals into homes and hopefully offer a reliable source of funds. Once we built a shelter, we would need that to cover our expenses.

We also needed to figure out how to set up free spay and neuter clinics in this remote location with no vet services for one hundred miles. Plus, we needed a plan to help families get access to vaccinations. Each year parvo was wiping out entire litters of puppies. A mass sadness that, with access to proper resources, can be prevented. Community outreach via a field team was on our checklist in addition to advocating for a change to the animal cruelty laws in our state and on tribal land.

All of those spokes were required to make the wheel go round if we wanted a healthier community for the people and the animals. But all of that was time consuming and costly. We were just volunteers that wanted to save animals and make a difference. Somehow, we'd have to figure it all out and find a way. I needed a sign that someone, somewhere, who came from nothing like us, had done it.

A very timely trip was in my future. I was about to get a firsthand look at the most successful animal rescue organization in the world. It was a trip that would break my heart, yet fill my cup and give me a renewed sense of why I needed to stick around.

If Keith and Dori could do it, so could I.

*https://news.nationalgeographic.com/2017/11/2017-hurricane-season-most-expensive-us-history-spd/

Lenny's Story

I was sitting at a high-top table tucked in the back of a brew house when my phone blew up with messages. By the overwhelming number of consecutive chimes I knew something was up that probably needed all hands on deck.

My husband and I try to get a date in each week—an hour of alone time where we put down our phones, tell bad jokes and catch up on each other's lives. I cut our date off mid-beer so I could help with Lenny.

"Honey we've got a gunshot dog," I said to my husband after a quick glance at what was going on. "I need to answer a few messages, okay?"

On any given day or night, volunteers—mostly Keith—will drop whatever is going on in their lives to do their part in the rescue chain. The following is a typical conversation at any hour of the day or night with a handful of volunteers on deck. Somehow through the cluster, head slaps, and heartaches, we always seem to get the job done and keep the garage rescue afloat.

We've got another gunshot dog coming in.

How bad is it?

Not sure, family said they saw him dragging his leg.

Is Keith available to pick him up?

I'll message him directly and see.

OMG, so sad you guys, I can't even take it.

I know, me too.

Just got a hold of Keith, he can be there in 30. Can someone get the 911 address?

I can.

Lady said a mile past the stop sign after the gas station then a few houses in.

That's her 911 address?

Yup.

I'll tell Keith.

Keith said he knows where it is.

He would. Lol.

What kind of dog? How big?

Black lab mix I think.

Do we have room for him?

Yes, Keith has one kennel open, but after this one we're full.

When is the next transport going out?

Not till Friday so when messages come in, we're full.

Got it.

Hey guys, a message just came in, a momma and litter of puppies is in this lady's outdoor doghouse. She said her dogs are freaking out and might hurt it if we don't get there soon.

Is Amanda free? Can she go get them?

Even if she can, where are we going to put them?
I don't know, we'll figure something out.

But Keith said he's full.

Guys I'm an hour away but I can get the puppies as soon as I get off work.

Thanks Amanda. You're the best.

Can someone get their 911 address?

Keith has the gunshot dog, it's bad. Drug his leg down to the bone. Said he'll be tied up all night with this one.

No one tell him about the puppies. We'll find somewhere for them.

Keith just messaged me and said that if we try to save this one, it will be thousands of dollars in vet bills. I'll throw up a post and start raising money. If we can raise enough, quick enough, then we don't need to talk about it.

Yes. Let's try to save him. Other than his leg, there seems to be nothing wrong.

Hey guys, I hate to even say it, but someone just messaged the page. She's asking if we can come get a stray or she threatened to call the dogcatcher.

Shit! We're over capacity big time. Even the outdoor doghouses are full.

Should we see if Amanda can go get him? I'll try to line up a foster for all of them for tonight.

Keith named the gunshot dog Lenny. The vet said he was shot in the back and that the bullet got lodged in his spinal canal, causing paralysis in one of his hind legs.

We don't know how long he had been dragging his foot but it was long enough to scrape it down to the bone. Lenny was in rough shape but we didn't ever discuss putting him ' down. A conversation that perhaps we should have had—a conversation that most rescues have to have.

We had to face this same question dozens of times over the years. How many times can we spend four thousand dollars on one dog? We'd recently saved Remington, could we afford to save Lenny too? Would we get enough in donations to do it again? How many dogs can four thousand dollars save instead of just one? We had policies in place for situations like this but we didn't have any hard-line rules. We had common sense and a goal to alleviate as much suffering as possible, but we also had heart. Since we functioned without any bureaucratic red tape to slow us down, we just did whatever we needed to do one day at a time.

I drank my craft beer and typed up a quick post about Lenny. It was a plea to our followers for help with what we knew would be a big surgery and recovery. Within just a few hours, an overwhelming amount of support and donations came in. Everyone told us to save him then pitched in ten or twenty dollars.

I cried that night. I was so grateful for how many people donated and saved Lenny. He looked so sweet, lovable and like a perfect family dog. Dogs like Lenny are the reason people in rescue end up with a zoo in their house and not a dollar in the bank. But in this case our followers stepped up and within a few days had donated more than four thousand dollars to put toward Lenny's vet bills. Every dollar over what Lenny's care needed stayed in a fund for future vet costs. The support was astounding. It motivated us to keep doing what we were doing. People we didn't know from all over the country were watching, pitching in and rooting for us to keep saving lives. We weren't about to let them down.

Keith drove Lenny three hours to a vet who was willing to do the difficult spinal surgery. The bullet was removed without complications, his leg was saved, but his paw was in tough shape. Lenny's prognosis was that he would eventually thrive without serious lasting injuries.

I don't know where Lenny is today, it's hard to keep track of all the dogs that go through Keith's garage. From the time they get picked up, to when they land in a permanent home, they can often go through a dozen or more hands and sometimes thousands of hearts that pitch in one or one hundred dollars to get them there.

Thanks to everyone who pitched in one dollar to save Lenny. He is alive because of all of you.

Check out Keith and Lenny at the beginning of Lenny's journey
http://bit.ly/LennysStory

CHAPTER TWENTY-ONE

Now That's Just Bull Pit

I lay on the twin bed that sat a few inches off the floor and scrolled through my missed messages and calls from the day. The smell in the air was unfamiliar, desert dusty mixed with a little doggie perhaps. But I didn't mind the unfamiliarity of it all because there was one thing that felt like home—the eighty-pound rock that lay across the bottom of my legs. The third eighty-pound rock that week. Each one different, yet each one the same. Night after night a beautiful stranger slept content at my feet and didn't move until the sun (and one ambitious rooster) woke us in the morning.

There is something about the rescue dogs here—they seem to know they made it out alive. They are overly respectful and by the way they look into your eyes you just know, they are grateful. Each one seemed to cast a subtle spell on me making it impossible to not feel the pain of their past, yet be hopeful about their future. We took a new one home each night to our rental house for a sleepover. This week they are all the same breed*ish*. Some blend of pit bull, or pitties, as my housemates call them.

They come from all over—high-kill shelters, busted fighting rings, neglect cases, surrenders. The time we spend with them helps get them adopted. They get to experience snuggles in a warm bed, a blanket on the couch with popcorn and a movie so that when their family arrives, they are acclimated to a normal life. These dogs are good citizens already and well-behaved for the most part. The trainers at the sanctuary work with them every day and it shows. Each just needs a home that is a good fit for their individual personalities.

On my first trip to the sanctuary I didn't know much about pit bulls. I knew Brenda had one, Utah, I'd met him a few times. He was a rowdy pup who could knock you over at full speed if you didn't get out of the way. He was also very well mannered, had a perky tilted head, and goofy smile. Besides Utah, I didn't know any other pitties. What I did know was that they were the most abused animal on the planet.

In 2008, the sanctuary took in the most famous group of pit bulls of all time. The group was dubbed, the Vicktory dogs. A name spun from the high-profile NFL player who funded the abhorrent dog fighting operation from where the dogs were rescued. Their plight from being forced to fight and enduring unthinkable abuse, to being rescued and living at the sanctuary is heartbreaking.

I was honored to be spending time at the organization skilled enough to take on their extreme case. Because of The Best Friends Animal Sanctuary and their success at rehabilitating the Vicktory dogs, rescued fight dogs now have a chance to live after being liberated from this inconceivable, torturous "sport." Before the successful rehabilitation of the

Vicktory dogs, United States law mandated that rescued fight dogs be euthanized regardless of their temperament, situation or age. The Vicktory dogs court case set a precedent that allowed skilled individuals to evaluate rescued fight dogs as individuals rather than implement mass "euthanize first, ask questions later" policy.

Two of the three ladies I've made the trip to the sanctuary with have pit bulls. They are also veteran volunteers. Brenda, Darcy and Penny are on a first-name basis with the tenured sanctuary staff. They are trusted with the dogs not all volunteers can handle and there seems to be some rule-bending for my friends from time to time. I was the newbie in the group. To my surprise, what I thought was going to be a week of hardcore animal training with face-eating pit bulls and poop shoveling around the clock, turned out to be a laid-back vacation snuggling with beefcake dogs.

Best Friends Animal Sanctuary is spread out over thirty-three thousand acres of Utah desert between Zion National Park and Bryce Canyon. Red cliffs speckled with sage bushes surrounded us on all sides as we drove toward the sanctuary each morning. I've never found the desert particularly beautiful or appealing but after a week of hiking through the brick red sand that is home to nearly six hundred rescued dogs, more than that in cats, plus dozens of pigs, goats and horses at any one time, I had a new, deeper respect for this desert.

Months earlier I'd asked Brenda what exactly we'd be doing at the sanctuary and I wasn't impressed with her answer. How can walking dogs and shoveling poo be meaningful rescue work? I get that it's grunt work, and I'm fine with grunt work. I can dig in and get dirty as good as anyone. I was just looking for something more meaningful.

How stupid of me to not consider the bigger picture. My initial assumptions were so wrong, my thinking so small. My time walking pigs at Piggie Paradise and mucking with Ron at Horse Haven turned out to be very important after all. Volunteers take a load off the resident caretakers, help to socialize the animals, and spread the word about rescue and adoption. I'm writing this book and talking about it now aren't I?

Over two trips I've had the privilege of interacting with dozens of animals that call the sanctuary home. I've taken pigs for a walk to help stretch their frail legs, legs that have been stunted in an attempt to keep them small for consumer demand. Creating a teacup pig is a cruel practice that causes extreme suffering. There is no such thing as a teacup pig. It is the term for a regular pig that should weigh three hundred pounds, but instead it's forced into a small crate and then kept on a starvation diet to keep it from growing. The toll this ignorant and inhumane practice has taken on their bodies is heartbreaking. It is my pleasure to take these pigs for a walk. If I had a hobby farm, I'd take them home.

That walk is as much for me as it is for them. It's important for me to feel in my heart that at least I tried to make a difference on this earth in whatever small way. Today I took a pig for a walk, showed that pig compassion, fed it a proper meal and cared for it like a good steward would. I feel good about that.

I realize my connection with the pigs is a bit stronger than most people would feel. I have advocated loudly for sixteen years about not eating them. Why we eat pigs and not dogs, cows but not cats, is a complicated cultural dichotomy. To me they are all the same, they are sentient. I would not eat a cow or a pig any more readily than I would eat my dog. For reasons that are lost to history, too many of us have become immune to seeing some animals suffer in cages but not others. We've become indifferent about the meat in our mouths. There is a more sustainable, humane way to satisfy an appetite.

My trips to Best Friends Animal Sanctuary have been joyful and sorrowful. What I take away from my time there is personal happiness. And a new, inspired outlook on this underappreciated world where humans fight tirelessly for the rights of animals. I've learned so much about the animal rescue world, the politics that surround it, and the emotional turmoil that is destined to be interwoven through it.

Volumes have been written on the miracle that is this organization. The Best Friends Sanctuary has much to teach the rest of the world about what a successful rescue organization can accomplish. They save tens of thousands of lives each year through their far-reaching network. Best Friends proves that no matter how big the problem, persistence is a solution. Until their No-Kill initiative, who could have believed that a world where no animals have to die in shelters could actually exist?

Since the launch of NKLA (No-Kill Los Angeles) a Best Friends Initiative that began in 2012, the number of pets killed in L.A. shelters has decreased by 82%. Quite simply, the goal of the initiative is to bring together animal welfare organizations and end the killing of homeless pets in L.A. shelters by providing spay and neuter services where they are needed most and increasing adoption rates.

In 2016, the NKLA Coalition adopted out about 26,500 dogs and cats and provided support for 14,050 spay/neuter surgeries. Los Angeles, the nation's second largest city, went from saving 71.3% of shelter dogs in 2011 to 91.93% in 2017, surpassing the initial no kill goal of 90%. The save rate for cats was even more remarkable at 36.3% in 2011 to 79.26% in 2017.

Large-scale adoption events, extensive marketing campaigns and community low-cost spay services can take much of the credit for the turn around. Now, Best Friends is taking this collaborative model and expanding it nationwide, leading an effort to take the United States to a no-kill status by 2025.

Starting in January 2019, under a new law, California will be the first state requiring pet stores to sell ONLY rescue animals. All pet stores will transition to selling dogs, cats and rabbits from shelters or adoption centers. Violators will be fined five hundred dollars for each animal that is not a rescue. Los Angeles is proof that if a city their size with a problem that seemed insurmountable just ten years ago can accomplish what they have, somehow, we can solve our problem too.

My trip to Kanab, Utah, came to an end and I had to go home to my family. I wouldn't be able to accompany Brenda any further down the rescue road for the time being. While I headed back to Fargo, Brenda headed to Texas. Her experience further highlighted that the problem is not isolated to the area TMAR serves. Assistance and money must come from outside those areas plagued by poverty if animal and human suffering is to end. We must find it within ourselves to close the gap between the haves and the have-nots.

Brenda's Story

Houston, You Have a Problem.

Fifth Ward Houston, Texas – Brenda

"I joined Alicia and Susan and began looking for homeless dogs to feed. It was 7 p.m. on the Friday of Memorial Day weekend and we didn't go more than a couple of blocks before we found homeless, hungry dogs to feed. Once we spotted a dog, we parked and then dumped a couple of ice cream-sized buckets of dry food on the sidewalk, topping it with several cans of wet food. Wet because it would provide some water since we weren't allowed to leave bowls. Sometimes as we're dumping food, more dogs came out so we create a second, third or fourth pile.

Alicia and Susan had an understanding with the residents that they wouldn't feed or approach dogs in fenced yards or dogs that were tied up. They weren't considered homeless even though they were often sick, starving, and left out in the elements. It was over one hundred degrees. Many of them had no food or water but help wasn't allowed.

We met people on the streets that were friendly but had very few resources for themselves. They had no ability to help the homeless dogs. As we pulled into one alleyway a man popped his head over the fence to inquire what we were doing. We told him about the feed run for dogs and he agreed to put out more food in a couple days and find some buckets for water for them. He had three dogs of his own inside a fenced yard that appeared to be cared for.

We stopped numerous times at locations where the dogs knew Alicia and Susan so they also knew a full tummy was coming their way. Dogs would come running from behind a fence surrounding the parking lot. At one stop a huge rat ran out, they shooed it away or it would eat the dog food. Everyone was hungry.

At an abandoned parking lot with tall weeds and grass, we stopped to try and find a dog they knew that hung out there. They repeatedly called to her but she didn't come. We searched the tall grass as there was an overwhelming scent of dead animal. We searched, but didn't find her body, and we never did see her alive. They were sure that her suffering had ended.

In the evening, many porches had large groups of people celebrating the holiday weekend. Loud music, laughter, raised voices, and interesting language filled the air. At some stops Alicia and Susan asked us N.D. gals to stay in the vehicle while they jumped out to feed dogs and chat with locals.

As we drove down a dark street, our headlights flashed on a couple of eyes. They were the eyes of a puppy whose face has stayed with me since that day. A lone puppy we gave some food and love to and then drove away. We did try to figure out how to take him with us. It was very emotional to leave him.

No, it wasn't emotional, it was heart-wrenching, completely messed up, totally shitty. It was so awful to have to fully grasp what we were doing. Shelters there were overflowing and euthanizing hundreds of dogs daily with many euthanizing all dogs under six months old. Alicia and Susan already had numerous dogs at their home and our vehicle had an unvaccinated mom with five, three-day-old puppies, plus another fourteen other dogs from Texas set to travel to North Dakota the next day. I was doing something I deemed unfathomable just hours earlier, but here, this was the reality of a feed run. We can't rescue them all . . . yet, and it totally freaking sucks. Bad.

I haven't figured out how to be okay with leaving that puppy behind and it's been months and months since that trip. I don't know how people like Alicia and Susan keep going back week after week, doing feed runs and leaving dogs behind that they've grown to love. Dogs who obviously love them not only for the food, but also for the love and attention they receive.

Alicia and Susan don't leave them all, they do move a lot of dogs into rescues. They post photos of the dogs in the Fifth Ward and will go back if a rescue agrees to accept them, otherwise picking them up and dropping them off at shelters means certain death.

A rescue we reached out to did step in to take the puppy the next day, but when they went back they weren't able to find him. Susan shared with me weeks later that she believes he was just away from his home and his owners found him that night. They took him into the safety of their home and gave him lots of love and a life he deserves. She creates a happy-ever-after to insulate her heart and maintain her spirit so she can keep doing what she's doing.

The next day as I prepared for the long trip back to North Dakota we saw a young, female pit bull come trotting through the parking lot. She was beautiful and all of my resolution had abandoned me. "Open your doors and let's get her in here." I no longer cared about doing what we should, I just wanted to save her. I wanted her to know love, kindness, a home. I wanted my broken heart to start mending by saving her. But we didn't save her. We gave her all the treats we had left and filled a lid with water and drove away.

We understand that if we take her and it upsets the residents, if she belongs to someone who just doesn't take care of her, we may undo what Alicia has done in building trust with this community.

The drive back was filled with many thoughts and few words. Things we saw, how we felt, what we did, what we didn't do. What we experienced, changed us all."

Follow Alicia McCarthy and Susan Hemmerich-Wetmore of The Forgotten Dogs of the 5th Ward Project for more on what they do and how you can help. http://forgottendogs.org/

CHAPTER TWENTY-TWO

TMAR Gets an Employee

I came back to town with a renewed sense of purpose and drive to push onward. Keith didn't seem to share my enthusiasm. I couldn't say I blamed him, dude seemed to have the worst luck. At times it felt like a black cloud of doom hung over his head alone, sabotaging everything he did. It was always one step forward, kennels clean, dogs fed, messages responded to. Two steps back, a new message about puppies outside in the cold, the litter in the garage has explosive diarrhea and the risk of parvo just went from green to red. Where would he put the litter that needed to come in from the cold without exposing them? What happens when there is just no more room?

The answer is one of two things. Either you can't save them, you tuck yourself into bed, try not to think about them dying and rationalize that what you've done will just have to be good enough. Or, you find a way to save them, all of them. The former saves humans. The latter saves animals. It does not go both ways. Something, or a part of someone, always dies.

Keith talked about moving south more than ever before; said how much he loved the south and missed it. He talked about buying land and just leaving town, starting over. Or how an island with no cell service, no people and no dogs would be a good fit. Keith was pretty much single now and doing everything himself. He had no job and therefore no income, no great prospects for work, and a dwindling life savings. He could live there without a job and in poverty for a few years but then what? He wouldn't have a dollar to leave town with, not one penny to put down on a home somewhere else, or even enough money for a rent deposit. There was talk about him running for Sheriff, or perhaps municipal judge. There was even talk of him going back to corrections. Everything was on the table, yet nothing was actually available.

A few of us girls talked on a private thread about what we would do without him leading the rescue. After a fundraiser we stayed to discuss worst case scenarios. How could we morph the rescue from being reliant on Keith to still doing the work without him? Who would be the boots on the ground? We didn't come up with any good solutions, only a pact between us that we wouldn't give up no matter what happened. Progress might slow, but we would somehow make it work. Amanda Marie Longie lived in the area TMAR served and helped as much as she could. She was fearless and motivated, maybe she could take over the day to day pickups? But again, a person with a full life and job taking on another full-time job didn't seem to be the best answer. We could recruit and find someone, but wait . . . where would they take the animals? There was no shelter. Would someone else be able to turn their garage and life into a rescue too?

We were put to the test with a message that shook us to the core. After so many events in the past year where we thought the rescue was over, or Keith was done, just when it seemed like things couldn't get any worse, Keith sent us a message.

I'm in the hospital. I think I had a heart attack.

At the time, I didn't know that most of the men in his immediate family didn't make it past the age of sixty. Apparently, almost everyone died of a heart attack. Keith told me that he never planned on living past sixty.

Ultimately, what seemed like a heart attack turned out to be symptoms of stress and severe burnout. Things were not about to get any easier. Sooner or later, the world breaks everyone.

> Rescue costs a lot. It was part of what ended my marriage. I'd be on the phone all night answering rescue messages and she'd say, "Can you put the phone down for a little while so we can spend some time together?" Sometimes I would, but other times I couldn't. She slogged through mountains of grunt work to save dogs. In the end, I chose the rescue over her, and that was shitty of me. She's a wonderful person, but sometimes you come to a bend in the path and you have to decide if you're going to go down it or not.

> Rescue can kill you. It can kill marriages and relationships. It just does. When she was here it was a lot easier. She did the real work of rescue. The unsung grunt work that nobody wants to do but has to be done for a rescue to function. The pounds and pounds of pee and poop picked up, the floor bleached and scrubbed, only to look like a painting done in

earth tones eight hours later. She did whatever was needed to save lives, she didn't ask for credit, didn't want it, and tried to stay out of the spotlight. She was humble but gave it 1,000 percent. I will always love her for who she is and what she did for these animals up here.

Rescue will chew you up and spit you out. Garage rescue is about not having a life, and that's what you have to adjust to. You have to accept that the hobbies, pastimes, and things you enjoy are going to go from 40 percent of the time to 4 percent. Your new hobby will be collecting dog poop and puppy pad origami. Even if you have a group of people it's not as bad, but it will always be a lot of work.

Wifeless and jobless, we felt more pressure than ever to take care of Keith and keep up with what he'd started. But the rescue couldn't afford a full-time employee if we ever wanted to build a shelter. Even if we could save money, how many years would hiring an employee set us back from building a shelter? Could he live on a few pennies each month until we could save up enough money? Then what? Go back to a job? Where, and doing what? We could not afford an employee. We could barely afford our monthly expenses and the van was on the fritz, again. Quite simply, without Keith there was no rescue, there would be no shelter, and no solution. We had to find a way to make it work. We needed to pay him to rescue animals full-time.

He had to be off the board of directors so we could hire him as an independent contractor. He could run the business as the shelter manager full-time and get paid. Keith said he would not take more than twelve-hundred a month. We told him he could not live on that, as it would barely be enough to cover his health care. He said he would not take one dollar more otherwise we would never have enough for a shelter. Basically, Keith volunteered to live in poverty for a year while we saved. He said he would chop wood, eat rice and ice fish to make it work. To shut him up, we agreed with him.

Five minutes later, in a conversation without Keith, the Angels committed to doing whatever was necessary to make this all work. We were in too deep to give up. We would find a way to pay Keith twenty-five hundred a month AND save for a shelter, AND cover all our monthly expenses. Whether we actually believed we could do it or not, we just decided to become unstoppable. It was the only way to win this war.

Winter was coming, and we knew what that meant. The cold and the death that was certain to follow would never end if any one of us gave up. Not only would each of us have to keep our head in the game, our game would have to get a lot better. I feared the worst; I might have to start going door to door. With that prospect in mind I wondered what else I could do to raise money… perhaps I could write a book?

Those first few winter months were exceedingly difficult. Keith had more dogs in his garage and house than anyone could manage and it was increasing by the day. The average intake seemed to climb by at least six individuals each week. He worked around the clock rescuing dogs, caring for them, doing the vet work he could do, making trips to the vet, cleaning kennels and cleaning kennels again.

Keith helped coordinate rescue placement, recruit

volunteers, recruit fosters and deal with vet bills. His personal washing machine had to work overtime day and night to keep up with soiled blankets and towels before it too, eventually broke. Pipes in the walls froze and one burst cutting off the water supply. Keith sent us a picture of a five-gallon bucket of snow sitting on top of his wood-burning fireplace—his only source of water for awhile. It might be better quality than the well water but was ten times the work to get if you included chopping wood for the fire, keeping the fire stoked and hauling a five-gallon pail of snow and water around. He truly did have the worst luck of anyone I'd ever known. Ever. He was broken, defeated and wanted to quit. But he never did. Keith is made of the stuff that builds empires.

I wrote about it. I cried about it. I posted what he was going through and the stories of the dogs that came through the garage. People pitched in more than ever before to help us pay Keith a salary. They pitched in for vet bills AND there was a little left each month to save for the shelter. As the Angels grew and more volunteers came on board, daily tasks were dispersed and fundraisers got thrown. Things were looking up. And down. For our new employee, like many other Americans, health insurance was an issue. He didn't have any, to be exact. And he needed basic care.

The Angels pushed on, saw an end in sight but at the burnout rate Keith was going we weren't sure he would be there with us at the finish line. We did everything we could to try to give him some semblance of a normal life. A day off, an hour, a moment of silence, a day without hundreds of messages to answer, one shift of cleaning. It wasn't much, or often, and more times than not his scheduled day off turned into a nightmare of impassioned volunteers making head scratching mistakes or arguing to the point where nothing got done. Everyone did the best they could under what was often emotional and stressful situations. Our rapidly growing rescue had turbulence but also perseverance and, well, a little crazy that kept us going. We were destined to have the highest of highs but also a few dark nights of the soul.

2017 was brutal. We saved so many but it still wasn't enough. Animals never stopped coming in. There were as many times where we felt hopeless as we did happy. Happy, it seems, can't erase a burdensome amount of tragedy. How much more tragedy can one person endure before they crumble into emotional pieces that can never be put back together? There is an actual term for what Keith and to a much lesser extent, some of the other volunteers, were experiencing.

Compassion Fatigue.

Apparently, it's a common affliction among animal rescue workers and healthcare professionals who work in the trenches. "Most people don't appreciate the strain this work causes," Patricia Smith, founder of the Compassion Fatigue Awareness Project, said. "Not only do (animal welfare workers) suffer daily in the work they do, they also often deal with the public's total disregard and criticism of their work. Shelter work was one of the most distressing and sorrow-filled work I've ever done."

An article published in *Psychology Today* explains: "No one likes to hear about the freezers full of euthanized animals. It's an uncomfortable reality, but often animal rescue workers have no option but to kill sick or badly wounded animals—as humanely as possible. For these professionals and volunteers, administering euthanasia is a major contributor to compassion fatigue—the chronic stress that stems from extended care giving. Combating the fatigue requires attentive self-care, and the ability to emotionally distance oneself from animal patients. But looking into the eyes of hundreds of distressed creatures day in and day out can make that difficult."

You become a rescue robot. I know people in the trenches know what I mean. You either find a way to keep going or you give it up like so many before. I want to give up all the time but I can't.

Garage Rescue means breaking plans or not bothering to make them. When you finally get caught up on all the messages and texts and think you just created a free hour to do something for yourself, a puppy needs saving. Yes, whatever you wanted to do was important, but not as important as saving a life. So you drop everything and go. The key to rescue, at least solo on the ground rescue, is not to get burned out. It's taken me many years and my marriage to get to that realization.

I had no plan on making this my life, it just happened. I woke up one day and I was the "Dog Rescue Guy." With that label comes all kinds of things I never would have thought of. It's not just going out and snatching a puppy from a crumbling shed. It's about dealing with people and not judging them based on your beliefs. It's about understanding situations that lead to animals needing help. It's planning buildings, being a vet for dogs that have no other option, managing personalities, picking up poop, feeding, cleaning and comforting.

To anyone that says caregivers fatigue isn't real, I have an ass you can kiss. There is only so much emotional energy to go around in a day. The single puppy that doesn't have a companion needs some attention. The two feral puppies have never had human contact for the first six months of their lives need some attention. The old dog, the injured dog, the neglected dog, they all need attention. My own dogs and the rescue cats need some attention. Between the feeding, watering, cleaning and messaging, you find time.

Then you sit down and look at the clock and it says 10:52 p.m. That's when you fit in time for you. Sometimes it is quiet, but most of the time you are awoken by the cat that walks past the one puppy that sees it and starts the chorus, *let me sing you the song of my people*. The young pups try to prove their bravery against the cat that couldn't give two shits they exist. The cat whose purpose in life has become to show his prowess by climbing the kennels at 5 a.m. Farley is often my arch nemesis. You give a cat a home with room, board, and food, and he might appreciate it, but he's a cat, and cats don't give a shit. But that's what I like about them.

Farley came into Keith's life when someone found him trapped in an abandoned apartment. He was left behind without any food and water. Not even the toilet lid was left up. Farley had been in there for about a week when he was discovered. Keith is allergic to cats so although he would try to help this tough feline, he'd have to move him along quickly. But when the team tried to find a home for the cat and weeks went by without luck, Farley grew on the big guy. Keith realized that Farley was not scared of dogs, at all. Farley roamed free in the garage alongside the kennels and in the house. He would scale the kennels to tease and taunt the dogs ensuring that a chorus of barking puppies and growling dogs never stopped.

Keith decided to keep him. Farley sits on top of the kennels while Keith is cleaning them, if the dogs go nuts, it's information about the dogs' demeanor toward cats that is helpful when trying to place them in the right homes. If the dogs couldn't care less about Farley, that's good info to know too.

Farley actually lifted Keith's spirits a little. He knocked things down, meowed endlessly on camera in the background of all the rescue videos and paraded himself in front of the newcomers at all hours of the night. Farley just did Farley and somehow Keith grew to love him. He would just need more allergy medication.

Keith not having health insurance, or knowing how to get it, let alone if we could afford, it was stressful. We had to get health insurance for him before we spent a dollar on anything else. We searched but nothing seemed to fit. Policies were expensive, one third of his yearly salary plus additional deductibles, copays, co-insurance and well, we felt like we just couldn't catch a break. We used all our connections to try and find something that would work. We explored options with family and friends who owned businesses, asking if they could put him on the payroll out of the kindness of their hearts. We'd give them an IOU and more than once each of us offered up what we would illegally do to get Keith covered. Those were not pretty or appropriate conversations but we were desperate. We talked about selling Keith, auctioning his virginity, but there were some problems with that. We'd sell a date with him, a week, we'd sell ourselves!

I wonder if all our sinful talk prompted what happened next? Maybe the devil himself heard us and decided that we were worthy of his fire and wrath so he started a real inferno. A fire in the engine of the rescue van, while Keith was driving, packed full with dogs.

There wasn't a volunteer among us that didn't pray even if they weren't the prayin' kind. We prayed for health insurance, a new vehicle, and for Keith to get a break—something, anything.

Eric and Rowdy must have been looking down, listening. They answered our prayers directly from heaven.

https://www.psychologytoday.com/us/blog/animal-emotions/201701/empathy-burnout-and-compassion-fatigue-among-animal-rescuers

CHAPTER TWENTY-THREE

Eric & Rowdy

They say bad things happen to bad people. If that's true, then I'm convinced that Keith was a serial killer in a previous life. I've never met someone with a bigger heart and more bad luck than Keith. If it could happen, it would, to Keith. He was on a sixteen-hour road trip to drop off more than a dozen dogs when I got the call. He was quite literally standing on the road.

"The van started on fire."

"What?"

"Just what I said. The van started on fire."

"Like, while you were driving it?"

"Yup."

"Everyone okay?"

"Yeah, we're all okay. It put itself out."

"Where are you? How are you going to get home?"

"I'm going to see if it'll restart and somehow make it there."

Which is exactly what he did. After that, the van had to be retired. When I got off the phone with Keith that day, I imagined him eight hours away from home with a van full of rescue dogs broken down on the side of the road, and I felt terrible for the conditions he was working under. He worked sixty to ninety hours a week and never seemed to have the proper equipment for the job. I had that all too eerie feeling that he was being pushed to his breaking point, again.

It was a miracle he made it back from even one of those trips in that old jalopy van. But the day it started on fire was the day us girls went to work on a new mission. This time we needed to get him a vehicle that didn't attract so much attention when he drove down the road, or catch fire. We joked on many occasions about how Keith must look to passers-by. A burly dude with a bushy beard in a rusted-out van with no windows, bumper held up with duct tape and wire. The van looked like it belonged in a horror movie, not something for transporting rescue animals.

We scrambled to figure out how to get him a suitable vehicle. We called dealerships, used our personal contacts and brainstormed. We decided we were going to throw some type of event to raise money specifically for a vehicle. In the meantime, I was going to throw up a post asking for a vehicle that could be donated, (in case someone had one lying around) you know, just in case. Then the most auspicious thing happened—from heaven. Literally from heaven, Eric and Rowdy heard our pleas and answered our call.

In 2011, Eric Halvorson, a man none of us knew, passed away at the age of thirty-two, leaving behind his wife, their two-year-old son and their dog Rowdy. He also left behind a 1999 Toyota 4Runner. It was an emotional donation the day his wife turned over the keys of that sentimental vehicle to TMAR.

The whole team cried tears of tragedy and generosity. We were beyond grateful. I reached out to Eric's wife Kim, to thank her personally. I asked her to tell me a little about Eric and Rowdy.

"Hi Charmaine,

Thank you for your email. I really enjoy talking about Eric so when it comes to him, I'm an open book. Please know that this donation is just as important for us, if not more, because it means something special is happening in memory of Eric and his best friend, Rowdy. So, thank you for accepting it.

Eric was a great man in many ways. One of his well-known traits was how much he loved animals. He was a sucker for a furry face. I held onto the vehicle for so long because at first I just couldn't bring myself to get rid of something that belonged to him. It has a lot of sentimental meaning to our family. I would drive it periodically and would take it to our annual camping event we hold in memory of Eric. When the time came that we were ready to part with the vehicle, I kept thinking how hard it would be to sell it to a stranger, so I really wanted it to go to someone special. After a couple ideas fell through, I opened up FB one Monday night and came across your post and thought, this was it!

It's an old vehicle and it definitely isn't perfect but it should last another 40,000 miles, so I hope it can help you, help those sweet animals.

It's the proper send off for a "special" vehicle. I didn't mention this to Keith, but March 17 had been our wedding anniversary and March 20 was Rowdy's birthday. So, the fact that we could donate it right between those two dates, cemented the idea in my heart that it was meant to be. Plus, after meeting Keith and the other volunteers, I knew we made a good decision. Thank you all so much for what you do for those animals, you definitely have our support!"

...

A picture of Eric from the obituary section of the newspaper lies in the glove box of the 4Runner where it will stay, forever.

Bella's Story

I've seen Keith in all sorts of situations from animal hoarding rescue to feral dog trapping. I have watched him crawl under just about anything you could crawl under to get dogs out. The most memorable of his field rescues, for me, is the one closest to my heart and home. Bella.

Two messages came in that week about porcupine dogs. Of the two dogs that day that had gotten themselves into trouble, the worst was the white Husky. He had been on our radar for a few weeks already. There were reports of a white, wolf-like dog seen along the highway with porcupine quills covering his head. Residents had been out looking for him, but like so many other shadow dogs they're scared, and easily disappear into the trees never to come out again.

Keith went to look for him. He did find that white Husky that day, but he still drove home with an empty kennel. The Husky lay in the ditch, someone had already put him down. One shot that ended his misery. The quills were extensive. Hundreds covered his head, eyes, mouth and neck. His wounds were infected and his starving body told the story of how long he'd been suffering. Later that week I got a message from Keith.

Going to be busy for a few hours.

What's up, need help?

No. Just what I wanted to be doing today. Pulling porcupine quills out of a pit bull's mouth.

He sent us her picture and photos of how she was doing as he pulled the quills. It was painful to see. The blood on the deck, blood covering his clothes. Her face looked like raw hamburger. Keith pulling those quills saved her life. He was the only option. There was no field vet or emergency weekend vet that could come. Even if there was, no one had the money to treat a case like Bella. Without his patience and compassion, she would have been put down on site. Which is why he was called out in the first place. Either to help or help put her down.

Her story is a testament to the dedication Keith has for saving animals. A bullet would have been much easier than an entire afternoon of pulling quills from a terrified pit bull. After, he took her back to the rescue to tend to her wounds. Over the next few weeks more quills came out of her head, mouth and throat. But something else was not right with her either. It was midnight when we got the message.

Bella's sick, I don't know what's wrong with her. It's bad.

I knew if Keith said it was bad, it was really, really, bad. Keith loaded Bella up in his truck and drove two hours in the middle of the night on a dark, country highway toward the nearest emergency vet. Because rescue never stops. Keith never stops. At times he wants too, but even then, he doesn't.

The vet said there was nothing they could do other than put her on different antibiotics, steroids, an IV and keep her overnight. She would be safe, but locked in a kennel with no one around. If she died, she'd die alone.

When we save a dog, we save it one hundred percent. That is the TMAR way. Keith took the medicine, then drove her home and gave her the IV himself. He would do anything he could to save her, but if she died, she would die in his bed, surrounded in love.

None of us thought Bella would make it through the night.

• • •

Six months later

My essay about Bella was published in the annual pet issue of a local magazine, *Fargo Monthly*.

Her demons come out at night. I don't know what she's seen or been through, but I know the night time scares her. When the shadows creep across our back lawn and the swings gently rattle, the tail that whacks me during the day out of pure joy falls somber and still at dusk. When she looks out the window and watches the tree branches come alive at night, Bella raises her hackles and a deep rumble emanates from her throat. I tell her it's okay and that she doesn't have to sleep outside in the cold ever again. She looks at me and smiles, walks over and sits down asking for comfort only I can give.

I'm her person. And she's my dog.

In the morning when the world is safe, her tail thumps

softly against the bed and the corners of her mouth curl up when I open one eye. If I open two eyes, she'll come over and greet me with a morning tongue bath. She loves me— A LOT. Well, maybe some of it is just separation anxiety but I don't care, it feels like love. She keeps the driver's seat warm for me until I get back and makes sure I'm never lonely while I pee. My life is so much happier with Bella in it each day, and each night I'm reminded that she is still adjusting to life as a family dog.

Bella is a rescue dog from Turtle Mountain Animal Rescue, the organization in North Dakota I have had the privilege to be a part of for going on three years. I wasn't looking for another dog when something in me spoke up and secretly wanted Bella. I'd been on a team that has moved thousands of dogs in the last few years, so why her? Why now? We already have a big dog, two little kids and a teenager. I didn't have a deep-rooted desire to own a beefcake pit bull-ish looking canine either.

So I guess The Dog Whisperer is right when he says, "You don't get the dog you want, you get the dog you need. "Being a part of her growth and recovery, seeing her spirit fill with joy as she runs and rolls through the yard and learning about her as an individual rather than a stereotyped breed has brought me a profound sense of happiness I never expected.

Someone asked me recently if I have regrets about taking her in, the hungry pit bull that tried to eat a porcupine and lived to tell about it. I thought about how our life has changed now that there are seven of us, and I couldn't come up with one regret. Bella has not been a burden or a troublemaker. She's a lover who is gentle with our little kids, mellow and unobtrusive then playful like a puppy. She's a good dog. A great dog. A perfect fit for us. Although she was definitely not what I was looking for, it seems she's just what I need. For me as much as her, rescue matters.

CHAPTER TWENTY-FOUR

The Business of Saving Animals

 After Kim's generous donation of Eric's vehicle, things really began to fall into place for the rescue. An angel donor stepped forward and guaranteed Keith's health insurance for one year. It was an affordable policy and we could continue it after that the year was up. We were contacted from people all over the nation.

From Washington to Maryland, we got messages of encouragement and support, letters from individuals who were brought to tears by the grass roots efforts of the team. Dozens of people we'd never met started "donating their birthdays" to the tune of thousands of dollars. One family threw a fundraiser and took entry fees for a game of beanbag toss and then donated a check for a nearly three thousand dollars. Businesses we'd never heard of from around the state and country sent us pay-it-forward checks and donated to our organization for their yearly charity events. Our savings, that we never actually thought would reach ninety thousand, was almost there.

We had our eye on some land for the shelter and Keith had blueprints drawn up. An architect donated a rendering we could use for events and a contractor was lined up, ready to go. Keith began to navigate the complicated issues of Tribal vs. State land and what we could and could not do. The pieces of the puzzle were laid out in front of us and slowly, one at a time they began to fit together. Our far off, insane, "you'll never build a shelter" dream was becoming a reality.

It was time to take everything TMAR did to the next level and get smarter about how we were operating the business of saving animals. Ninety percent of the dogs that went through Keith's garage would end up on an eight-hour journey to a sleepy town in northern Wisconsin—a town with a big heart, Coco's Heart. The rescue organization that took in almost all of the TMAR dogs for the first few years of operation and adopted out every single one of them. A huge success and no easy feat. There were no other shelters that could handle the volume of dogs we rescued except Coco's. They were pivotal in the placement of thousands of TMAR dogs over several years. We did everything we could to get the dogs there. That didn't happen without cost. Transportation from northern North Dakota to Wisconsin was setting us back up to three thousand dollars a month. From a business perspective, it was not a smart move, nor was it sustainable. At the time we had no other option. As we moved forward and continued to grow, we were going to have to figure something else out.

There were at least ten solid volunteers now, each as motivated as the next. Plus, we had a dozen or more individuals who would do occasional transports or foster care. It was still small, but it was growing network. Krista Majkrzak, an acquaintance of mine from years ago, serendipitously joined the team and was central in taking the transport, foster, and rescue-to-rescue divisions to a new, more organized level. We went from driving dogs to one location in Wisconsin to working with a dozen local shelters—a much more efficient and cost effective system. Our straight-line rescue model sprouted branches and was expanding rapidly throughout the mid-west.

Kim Gordon joined the team and whipped our daily chaos into shape in an impressive amount of time. She stepped in everywhere she could and took on the supreme task of seeking out and writing grants. A necessary, complicated, and time-sucking process that would help to ensure our long-term survival.

Trista took on the feline problem and made it possible for us to take litters of kitties into foster care. Soon after, she began working with the national chain PetSmart, who would help us adopt out TMAR cats.

Aliah took the lead for fundraising and before long we had events popping up all over the state bringing in money that would sustain us for months at a time.

I began to put together an adoption division with the goal of adopting out ten dogs each month. It took months of planning and recruiting a team; putting paperwork and policies in place. In the first month, we did home visits with dozens of families and adopted out fifteen dogs. The first was Luna, whose family drove all the way from Montana to Fargo to get her. Now she spends her days as an unofficial employee at Yellowstone National Park. Everyone pitched in anywhere that was needed. Keith called us Angels 2.0.

A few months into the summer of 2018, I turned over all adoption duties to volunteer Andrea Ley Coombs, who doubled my goal within a month and adopted out more than thirty TMAR dogs! The right people have come to TMAR at the right time, causing more pieces of the puzzle to fit together.

A couple from Fargo, Ellery and Chad Lystad, stepped in and turned their lives upside down to take in TMAR dogs every night of the week for months on end and of their own volition, they began to organize fundraisers. Their contribution has been invaluable. Katie Kapocious lost her mind but eventually found it again while helping Krista find enough foster families to support the one hundred dogs coming in each month.

Those are only *some* of the volunteer contributions. Each foster family, individual transporter, independent rescuer, or donor is a vital cog in the rescue wheel who will probably never get the credit they deserve. There are friends and neighbors all over the country that, without them, fostering, transporting or fundraising, TMAR would not be the lifesaving machine it is today.

In the next six months the team doubled in size again. Shannon, Sandra, Jessica, Angie, Annette, Joey, Jamie, Erin and a handful of others work each day behind the scenes keeping everything afloat. Some volunteers would stay, some would go, but TMAR turned a corner.

Keith still had bad luck and burnout on an almost daily basis, which can mostly be attributed to lack of help on the ground in his garage, but the bigger picture of our rescue mission was coming together. He would be able to hang in there long enough to build a shelter and move the rescue out of his garage.

The 4Runner was great for local pickups and transports but could only hold one large kennel. To be efficient and move more than a dozen dogs at a time, we needed a van. If someone could donate a 4Runner then maybe someone had a van lying around? Never hurts to ask, right? But no one had a van to donate from heaven that time. We started a campaign with a photo of Keith next to the old one. Keith looked like a vagabond at best, kidnapper at worst. Within a few weeks between beer house events and online fundraisers, we raised ten thousand dollars. Not quite enough for a cargo van that wouldn't break down, but close enough for a car company based out of Devils Lake to step in and help.

Bergstrom Cars caught wind of our story and donated the rest of the money we would need for a brand new, white cargo van. Upon delivery, they generously put our logo on the side and filled it with supplies. The outpouring of support and generosity for TMAR has been nothing short of miraculous.

So what do you do with an old white van that you no longer have a use for? You fill it with explosives, invite your friends over for a bonfire and pass out your arsenal of guns. What else would you do?*

---

*This may or may not have happened. Just sayin'.

Losing Bubba

You have to make the call that's best for them, NOT what's best for you.

I felt like shit with Bubba. I didn't want to do it because he had maybe another three months left. But it was three months of slowly going downhill. Should I put off the pain a little longer? The pain of letting go because by the time he was miserable the choice would be easier? As family members we owe them more than that. Showing them love doesn't mean prolonging things because you can't deal with it. I know that might hit a nerve with some, but in the grand scheme of easing suffering, you're not helping them. You're only helping yourself by keeping them around past their time.

After it was over I went inside, lay on the couch and cried. I read replies to the post about Bubba's life and his last day and cried some more. My Facebook people helped me grieve. I live alone up in the woods, no neighbors, but I had strangers from around the country that cared enough to write kind words. It helped me to get it out so I could move on.

You have to move on in rescue.

Acknowledge, accept, deal, move on.

That's how you keep going.

I've always believed that the death of a pet can be more painful than the death of a human. Losing a family member is devastating, but losing the family member that sleeps in your bed every night, wakes you up every morning with a smile and a wag is unspeakable. Still, with as much as we love them, their love for us is immeasurably, more unconditional. An incredible thought to ponder—how can they love us so deeply, with so much abandon and forgiveness? Imagine what humankind could accomplish with such resolve.

The loss of Bubba was devastating on all of us at the rescue. I cried for days leading up to his death and more in the days after. Even though I'd only met Bubba a handful of times, I think I mostly cried for Keith. I know what it feels like to lose a companion. But it was Keith who suffered the additional trauma of being the one who mercifully ended Bubba's life.

Over the three years that I've known Keith, I've asked him about having to put dogs down. There have been some hard, but enlightening conversations ending in ways I never could have expected. Each conversation gave me a little more perspective and a lot more respect for the man who has saved thousands of lives but who has also ended a handful too.

Keith's emotional goodbye to Bubba. bit.ly/LosingBubba

CHAPTER TWENTY-FIVE

No-Kill TMAR

Rescue is a game of numbers. A series of chess moves you must get right if you want to save as many lives as possible. Sometimes those chess moves require God-like decisions no one wants to make. But someone has to make them because without them, there is no rescue.

TMAR has to play the numbers game too. How do you save as many lives and eliminate as much suffering as you can? Sometimes that means making heartbreaking decisions. Sometimes dogs have to be put down. A friend of mine who works closely with a rescue in a different town told me that every time the board votes to euthanize one of the animals, they lose at least one volunteer. As infrequent as it is, it's never an easy decision under any circumstances. TMAR is not immune to the same difficult issue either. Luckily, it is rare for us to be in that situation.

TMAR has a proven, impeccable track record for saving animals and not euthanizing them. The current benchmark for no-kill status among animal shelters is saving 90 percent or more of the animals who enter that shelter. The benchmark for entire cities to have no-kill status is saving 90 percent or more of the animals held collectively in shelters city wide. From its inception until now, TMAR has had to euthanize less than 1 percent of the animals rescued.

The 1 percent that have been euthanized or died after they were in our care were too ill or injured to survive. An even smaller number had known severe behavioral concerns with documented human bites, or fatal attacks on other domestic animals. These few dogs are deemed a substantial risk to the public including all TMAR volunteers, transporters, fosters, and Keith.

There are rescues scattered across the nation that have 80-150 dogs a day dropped off at their facilities. Hundreds of thousands of dogs get euthanized each year in shelters because there is no room. Luckily, we have never had to put an animal down for that reason. Through incredible effort, we've always found room. We also don't have to take in 150 dogs a day like some cities in the southern states. They are the ones faced with unthinkable choices each day. In rescue, there is no room for criticism.

Big Chief's Story

Everyone wants to be a
lion. Until it's time
to do lion stuff.

-Unknown

So today sucked. I had to put Big Chief down this morning. I didn't want to do it, and I felt bad, but it was what was best for him. It's like having to put your own dog down every time you do it. You have to walk past the kennel he was in just hours before, you have to not think about it to keep going, but it doesn't always work that way. These are the situations nobody wants to hear about. "I'm so sorry, I don't want to know, it's just too sad." But that's what real rescue is. It's moments when you are sitting watching TV trying to take your mind off the fact that you're going to have to put the puppy in the garage down.

Big Chief was hit by a car and the people simply couldn't afford the vet bill. It's the unfortunate reality of where we live. If the dog isn't suffering so bad that it has to be put down right there, I bring it home and try to give it a chance. Big Chief wasn't going to make it no matter what. I had to put animals down when I was a deputy. A world where a vet was instantaneously available to end suffering would be such a relief. That's not the way it is, especially not here. I hate doing it. I absolutely hate it. I do the best I can. I sit with them and pet them. I talk softly to them and do everything I can to comfort them. This way the last thing they know is love.

I've rushed badly injured dogs to the vet and it's horrible. Every bump, twist and turn causing more suffering because you have to drive fast. So now I have to decide. Do I take this broken puppy down the bumpy road to the steel table, or do I go sit with him and comfort him for an hour and then he's gone in an instant while eating bacon?

I know I will have PTSD some day from it, if I don't already have it now. But for now I need to eat it. I need to do what's best for him, not my feelings or someone else's opinion. Then only I have to deal with it, I have to try and burn it out of my head and forget it ever happened. It's the only way to keep going. I send a message out to the team and say I had to put Big Chief down. I don't want to talk about it. Please don't say sorry or anything else. It's because I need to make the memory go away. It breaks my heart every single time I have to do it, but I have to do what's best for them. My world of rescue is about easing suffering.

I want that to be where every dog finds a happy home, and gets treated and healed no matter what, but what I want and what has to happen are two different things.

CHAPTER TWENTY-SIX

A New Code

In September of 2018, Keith formally proposed the following changes to the animal welfare laws on the Turtle Mountain First Nation. This was the original tribal code.

"Tribal Code 26.1104 Cruelty to Animals: Any person who shall torture or cruelly mistreat any animal, or fail to take proper care of any domesticated animal, shall be guilty of a Class 1 offense."

It was vague and thoughtless—yet a paragraph that shockingly, put the state of North Dakota's laws to shame. The state laws include everything above and nothing more but give further detail that exclude nearly everyone on the planet from being persecuted from those laws.

The proposed changes were submitted by Keith to the tribal council on several occasions. The most recent of which seems promising. Local TMAR supporters called their council members asking them to support the proposed changes. Those calls apparently lit up phones and blew minds. The outpouring of support was beyond the norm. The new animal protection laws are as such. (*If you aren't interested in reading them. Let me summarize: They don't suck.*)

Any person who shall torture or cruelly mistreat any animal or cause any dog to fight with another dog shall be guilty of a Class 2 offense. For purposes of this chapter, "torture or cruelly mistreat" means: (*a*) breaking an animal's bones, (*b*) causing the prolonged impairment of an animal's health, (*c*) mutilating an animal,, and (*d*) physically torturing an animal. For purposes of this chapter, "dog fight" means causing any dogs to injure each other, for amusement or gain.

A law enforcement officer may take custody of an animal if the officer has probable cause to show the animal has been abused. Upon seizing an animal the law enforcement officer shall provide care for the animal, either directly or through a contractual arrangement with another person. For purposes of this subsection, "care" means food, water, and shelter from the elements, as appropriate for the species, the breed, and the animal's age and physical condition, and necessary medical attention. If convicted of violating this chapter, the owner of an animal seized under Code 26.1104 is responsible for all costs related to the animal's seizure, including required notifications, attorney's fees, court costs, and any costs incurred in providing the animal with care or in providing for its destruction in accordance with section 26.1104.

Add Neglect as a Level 1 offense. A person shall be guilty of the Class 1 offense of neglect if there is a failure to provide any domesticated animal with

1. food and water, shelter from the elements as appropriate for the species, breed, and the animal's age and physical condition;

2. necessary medical attention if the animal is visibly suffering or has obvious significant injury that has not been attended to; and

3. an environment that is free of conditions likely to cause injury or death to an animal of that species, breed, age, and physical condition. If the dog is chained or held in place by a similar mechanism, the area must be kept sanitary enough that no more than 40% of the available area be covered in feces, and a chain length of at least 10 feet.

A law enforcement officer may take custody of an animal if the officer has probable cause to show the animal has been neglected. Upon seizing an animal the law enforcement officer shall provide care for the animal, either directly or through a contractual arrangement with another person. For purposes of this subsection, "care" means food, water, and shelter from the elements, as appropriate for the species, the breed, and the animal's age and physical condition, and necessary medical attention. If convicted of violating this chapter, the owner of an animal seized under Code 26.1104 is responsible for all costs related to the animal's seizure, including required notifications, attorney's fees, court costs, and any costs incurred in providing the animal with care or in providing for its destruction in accordance with section 26.1104.

These changes turn shoddy guidelines into commonsense laws that protect sick, starving and abused animals. Under the new code, law enforcement and TMAR would work together so that cruelty and neglect cases can be brought to court. Animal cruelty cases on tribal land are routinely not prosecuted because there is nowhere to hold the animals until trial. For the cases that Keith was involved in while he was a deputy (like Bubba's story) he held the animals at his private residence. Unless an officer is willing to do that, there is no case. Under the proposed changes TMAR would work with law enforcement to hold those animals, or find placement for them while a case is pending.

Unfortunately these laws have not passed, yet. But we are confident that the tribal council will follow through and with a little negotiation there can be a workable outcome for everyone. Both sides agree that we are not on opposing teams. We are working together to make changes that are for the betterment of every living being. Bridges have been built and are being crossed both ways. This is a success.

When these laws do pass, they will be unprecedented. The Turtle Mountain Tribe is about to pave the way for other First Nations to do the same. The laws have been written, a model of rescue has been established that can be taken to other tribal lands.

Hudson's Story

An urgent message about a stray just came in. Sounds bad. Amanda should be able to go get him. She should be there shortly.

Once Amanda was on the scene, Keith messaged on the team thread.

Is he breathing?

He's extremely scared and in pain. He's breathing but his neck is absolutely horrendous.

Do you have time to get him to the vet? Tell Bottineau or Rugby to bill the rescue.

Okay I'll call the vet. You can smell his flesh, it's so bad.

None of us know exactly what happened to him. Perhaps he ran away and had been living as a stray for months and no one was around to loosen his collar as he grew. Perhaps something more sinister happened, we don't know. Until Hudson, I was completely unaware there was even a term to describe his condition.

We were all waiting patiently on standby to hear how he was doing. Amanda sent videos of him while they were at the vet. What I saw made me feel sick in my stomach and sticks with me still today. I'd never heard of or seen an "embedded collar." From the look of his injuries, he must have been in so much pain. I was relieved they sedated him immediately. From there he was under constant care and pain killers until he healed.

I was thrilled to have tracked down his family and see how he's doing today. He lives with a wonderful woman, Sandra Bernard, her other dog Elway and two cats. Sandra says they are all very attached to each other. On Hudson and Elway's first night together, they bonded and have been inseparable ever since. Sandra works from home and said Hudson spends all day outside in her big back yard stalking squirrels. It is a personal pleasure of mine to watch Hudson's journey when Sandra posts pictures and updates on her Facebook. His eyes look happy, his coat shiny and healthy, each time I see him it brings on happy tears.

When Hudson got to Sandra, he had a hard time meeting new people but she said he eventually began to trust humans again. Now Hudson enjoys meeting new people without any issues. His wounds, inside and out, are healed.

"We are just overjoyed and blessed that we can provide a forever home to such a wonderful dog." – Sandra Bernard

Some of Hudson's intake photos and videos can be found here. http://bit.ly/HudsonsStory

CHAPTER TWENTY-SEVEN

North Dakota, You're Next

The world is a dangerous place to live, not because of the people who are evil, but because of the people who don't do anything about it.— Albert Einstein

I grew up in Fargo, North Dakota. The gravel roads turned into a hopping suburban sprawl with more jobs than people, and bigger salaries than anywhere else in the state. There are big yards here, brick homes and voracious appetites for food and liquor. For the most part, if you are willing to work, there are plenty of jobs and money.

In a study published by *Forbes* magazine, Fargo was ranked the best small city in the nation to start a business or career. According to a 2018 article in *USA Today*, Fargo also ranks as the fifth drunkest city in America. Life here, although cold and isolated at times, is pretty cushy and apparently also pretty drunk.

North Dakota has made its mark in recent years for the oil behind the boom, the way in which we frack it and how to transport it. From small town creeks where water burns with fire to the now widely publicized Standing Rock revolt against DAPL (Dakota Access Pipeline). The media coverage on issues all across the Dakotas has kept the broadcasting professions at work. We have boomtown coverage, sex trafficking, oil fracking, First Nation protests, stand offs and murder. Yet, there is one issue that has not been in the press as much as the more glamorous "man camps" and "pipeline protests."

North Dakota has some of the most lax animal cruelty laws in the Nation. A report by the Animal Legal Defense Fund (ALDF) ranked North Dakota among the "worst five" states for animal rights laws. According to an article published in Newsweek in March of 2018, "For the 11th year in a row, Kentucky was ranked the worst of all the states for animal protection laws, followed by Iowa (49), Wyoming (48), Utah (47) and North Dakota (46)."*

According to the Bismarck News in January 2017, "North Dakota—again—ranks near the bottom of the Humane Society's rankings for states with the weakest animal protection laws. The state ranks 48th." The Humane Society looks at ninety-three policy ideas that range from animal fighting, cruelty and wildlife abuses, to fur and trapping. North Dakota has been in the bottom four of the Humane Society's ranking for states with the weakest animal protection laws since the rankings began. I am saddened that we can't have commonsense anti-cruelty laws in my state.

The exact problem with the laws here is that what regulations do exist (which aren't terrible) just don't apply to anyone. On the www.nd.gov site, the laws look pretty straightforward with common language for abuse, neglect, abandonment, etc. But, look closer and you'll see that those laws don't apply to everyone. There is a long list of exemptions. A clear case of cruelty, neglect, abuse or abandonment would not be a case at all if the owner was able to be categorized under one of the many exemptions. The state would like it to seem like the laws are comprehensive and protective, but in actuality, because of the exemptions, they rarely apply to anyone. If we read the laws as they are actually written, *including the exemptions*, they would sound like this.

In North Dakota with respect to dogs and cats, it *is permissible* to willfully engage in animal neglect including not providing adequate food and water, not providing shelter from the elements or giving necessary medical attention, an environment free of conditions likely to cause injury or death to that animal are acceptable, if the animal is a part of one of the "usual and customary practices" as long as that neglect, abuse or cruelty is a part of one of the categories below.

1. The production of food, feed, fiber, or ornament, including all aspects of the livestock industry

2. The boarding, breeding, competition, exhibition, feeding, raising, showing, and training of animals

3. The sport of rodeo

4. Animal racing

5. The use of animals by exhibitors licensed under the Animal Welfare Act

6. Fishing, hunting, and trapping

7. Wildlife management

8. The culinary arts

9. Lawful research and educational activities

10. Pest, vermin, predator, and animal damage control, (b) the humane or swift destruction of an animal for cause, and (c) services provided by or under the direction of a licensed veterinarian.

Additionally, in North Dakota it *is permissible* to willfully engage in animal abuse (Class A misdemeanor for a first *and* second offense) classified as any act or omission that results in physical injury to an animal or that causes the death of an animal if that animal is also a part of the "usual and customary practices" listed in 1-10 as stated above.

Meaning, abuse will not be prosecuted if the abuse happens within one of the exemptions. Furthermore, the same exemptions apply to the laws outlining animal cruelty (a) breaking an animal's bones, (b) causing the prolonged impairment of an animal's health, (c) mutilating an animal, or (d) physically torturing an animal. North Dakota attorneys are not able to prosecute if the act of cruelty falls under one of the many exemptions listed above. Feel sick to your stomach yet? Me too. Don't believe me? Check it out for yourself at www.nd.gov.

North Dakota also does not have laws that require counseling for animal cruelty offenders nor do we require a person charged with animal cruelty to cover the costs of caring for the animals involved. I did some digging into a law proposed in 2017 titled HB 1301 that would have made it so taxpayers no longer had to cover the costs and enable convicted animal abusers to get away with their crimes without having to be financially responsible for that animal. In other words, a convicted animal abuser does not have any financial responsibility for the care of that animal.

North Dakota lawmakers killed the bill with a ten to four DO NOT PASS for reasons that are beyond my comprehension. In a videoed segment of the vote, it took less than one-minute for lawmakers to decline to protect animals and taxpayers while enabling animal abusers.

So, what do you do when you're an advocate for animals, born in North Dakota and have some time on your hands after your next book releases? You make noise, rally, petition, write, call, and organize a movement to change those laws in your state and abroad.

Myself, Keith, the volunteers at TMAR, plus thousands of other advocates in the animal rescue community are working together to campaign for tougher laws in North Dakota, other states across the country and on First Nations. We understand that rescue matters, adoption, education and spay and neuter matters. People who are struggling, matter. Laws matter too, and if enforced could have a lasting positive impact on the welfare of animals in the areas that need help the most.

Email cjenglishauthor@gmail.com to be notified about how you can participate with us in this movement.

Volunteers will be doing everything from sending an email, making a phone call, and giving a signature, to showing up at a peaceful protest.

We will do nothing more and nothing less than using our bodies and voices to stand up for animals who do not have a voice. I'm all for thoughts and prayers, but I'm more for policy and change.

*https://www.newsweek.com/animal-cruelty-which-state-worst-protecting-animals-855098

Hope's Story

The two resident dogs that occupied the doghouse had not been friendly to strays. Why they allowed Hope to come in can't be explained. Hope lay down and gave birth. By morning the little, wooded house had eight additional occupants. When the family realized what happened, they called Keith.

Hope was a feral dog and completely untrusting of people. If Keith scared her away she might not survive the extreme temperatures and with her gone, bottle-feeding one-day-old puppies would be an extreme undertaking with all sorts of unknowns that put their chances of survival at significant risk.

Keith crawled into the doghouse and found Hope standing over her puppies growling and showing her teeth. He talked to her with a kind voice and she eventually stopped. Another thirty minutes later, Keith knew he had no choice. He had to get her out. It was for her own good, and for that of her puppies.

When he drug her out she fought hard, tried to chew through the lead, rolled on the ground like an alligator and stepped on one of her pups. Keith got bitten on the arm and leg but used it as opportunity to grab Hope, bear hug her and get her into the kennel. Then he went back for her puppies.

> Something bad happened to her at some point in the past. She made the decision she was not going to deal with humans ever again. When I got her back to the garage, she wouldn't let me get the slip lead on her so I had to use the catch stick. I absolutely hate the catch stick with every piece of my being. She was rolling, shitting, snarling and screaming. I had to drag her through the garage, she bit, broke her tooth and started bleeding. I felt like total shit doing it, but it's what I had to do to try and save her.

Once inside the garage kennel, she didn't move for twenty-four hours. She lay on her stomach with her head in the corner. She was literally frozen and scared for an entire day and wouldn't roll onto her side for the puppies to nurse. Hope was terrified every time Keith approached.

One of the pups was not doing good. Something was wrong with its back legs and it was not near the others and didn't try to nurse. When Keith picked it up it was stiff, frozen. He took it in the house, carried it around tucked under his armpit, gave it a warm bath, dried it with the hair dryer then kept it under his shirt.

> Sometimes with puppies they come back, it looks like they are frozen solid, but they come back.

After forty-five minutes it was moving around and crying a little, he tried to give it formula but it wouldn't take a bottle or milk from a syringe. It aspirated everything. He laid the puppy next to Hope but it wouldn't nurse. The puppy didn't make it through the night.

Keith couldn't send Hope along the rescue chain if she couldn't be handled. She wasn't mean or aggressive, she was scared and had been severely abused. Keith made the decision to let Hope stay at the rescue with him. He let her occupy one of the valuable kennels where others could have gone. She stayed at the rescue for months while he worked to rehabilitate her.

Slowly she began to trust him. When he wasn't around, she would peek her head out of the kennel and look around the garage then sniff. Eventually she came out on her own (when he wasn't around.) He left the house door open for her so she could go inside. Because of pizza crust and a whole ton of patience, Keith and Hope are now friends with a mutual respect enough to co-exist peacefully. Hope has been at the rescue with Keith for about a year. At one time Keith's personal pile of dogs consisted of Val, Bubba, Bella, Bear, Hope, and Farley, the cat. But since I had taken Bella, and Bubba had recently passed, keeping Hope as one of Keith's dogs wasn't as much of a burden.

Our followers fell in love with Hope as much as we did. Her journey from day one is documented on the TMAR Facebook page. My personal favorite memory is Hope at Easter dinner. Instead of being a polite houseguest Hope pooped in the middle of the kitchen floor.

Here is a video of Hope and her pups not long after she came to TMAR. www.bit.ly/HopesFirstWeekAtTmar

And Hope's Easter dinner surprise. http://bit.ly/EasterDinnerSurprise

CHAPTER TWENTY-EIGHT

Determined Rescue Seeking Permanent Shelter

The county's offer was to put up a building we could use as a shelter under the terms that we could lease and pay rent each month, which also meant that the contract was at the whim of future politicians who may or may not support our cause. There was no guarantee our lease would be renewed and there was also no guarantee that when leadership seats changed hands, we wouldn't get kicked out of the building or have it re-purposed for something else. This was not our vision. When we do something, we do it all the way.

What they were offering was what we were already working with, except we'd have to pay rent. We already had a makeshift building not meant to be a rescue with inadequate ventilation, no access to outdoor runs or commercial laundry. It would be unwise to swap one insufficient building for another with the same problems. It was not a good deal for TMAR, the communities we serve, and the supporters that donate their money to the cause. Thank you. But no, thank you.

If we were going to move out of Keith's garage and into a shelter we would do it right and make it a place the community could permanently have as a resource. A shelter with a sterile room for round-the-clock spay and neuter, a quarantine area, a place where once we had the problem under control, if properly managed would never get out of hand again. We were going to stick to Keith's vision.

> Our goal is to make a positive impact, not only for the animals, but the youth of the community as well. We plan to establish a program where kids can take part in the rescue and rehabilitation of animals while learning positive life skills to help build self-esteem, pride, and responsibility.

This is where I'd love to tell you that we built that shelter and it's magnificent! Not too big, but with adequate room and supplies and a community area where kids can come and help. We're close, but we're not there yet.

There are many pieces in place. But everything that must happen from buying the appropriate land to having a water well dug to the actual construction of the building itself, is a monumental task. Keith and team continue to move seventy to one-hundred animals each month along the rescue chain. There is no time for anything else and we still run into problems on a daily basis that set us back in time, and money. So yes, we are still operating out of Keith's garage, our cars, our homes and our hearts. But this is not failure nor a permanent situation. We will build that small, yet incredibly necessary shelter.

I was going to wait and write this story after we built a shelter.

I was going to wait until after we hosted ten free spay and neuter clinics and were no longer taking in one hundred dogs a month because there was not one hundred a month to rescue.

I was going to write this story when the ending was done.

Then I realized our efforts will never end. Once we hit a milestone, we will push on toward the next one. We are a success with or without a shelter—a story worthy of being told now and in the future.

Keith and the volunteers at TMAR have inspired people from around the nation to support animal rescue, adoption and no-kill initiatives. Individuals who have never heard of Turtle Mountain or perhaps even North Dakota, stepped in to support our efforts. People everywhere have helped the invisible dogs become seen. We have made a difference that will last for generations to come—saved tens of thousands of lives from being born onto a land that cannot support them.

If there is a moral here, it is that we as individuals cannot stand by and watch, we must act. If we don't, more animals will suffer and die from the death of our inhumanity. Rally, gather, fight back, speak loud, get up and do something about it if you want it to change. TMAR is proof that you don't need a government or law to change the lives of thousands of animals. All you need is some grit, heart and the will to persevere. Beat the drum until you wear it thin, then replace it and start your chant again.

Glory's Story

 I've heard people say that when we get to heaven we'll be greeted by all the animals. That the ones we've loved and lost will be there waiting for us in the end. I don't know if that's true. I hope so. If it is, the team will have their arms and hearts full of fur and their faces thoroughly licked when they get there.

Especially by Glory.

He loves kisses. Glory was ten weeks old when he got to the garage. He had multiple skin infections, mange, conjunctivitis, worms, and was severely dehydrated and near death from starvation. We often don't know where they were born or how they came to be seen, we focus on moving them on to a better life.

Keith gave him medicated baths to soothe his raw skin and now that he knows humans are not the enemy, he has begun to thank us. With kisses. Lots of kisses. We promised Glory that the world he'd come from would never hurt him again and we will keep our promise.

A kind man named Chad surrendered him and our volunteer, James took him in and named him, then Keith took over. After Keith he went to Jennie, where she fostered him for weeks until he was ready for the next leg of his journey.

Here is the video of Keith and Glory on his first night at the rescue.
http://bit.ly/GlorysStory

2829.2830.2831.2832.2833.2834.2835.2836.283
7.2838.2839.2840.2841.2842.2843.2844.2845.2
846.2847.2848.2849.2850.2851.2852.2853.2854
.2855.2856.2857.2858.2859.2860.2861.2862.28
63.2864.2865.2866.2867.2868.2869.2870.2871.
2872...

....

....

....

....

....

....

....

....

....

....

....

....

....

....

....

....

....

....

....

....

..................................3999.

Keith began rescuing animals in 2013. A formal shelter count for TMAR didn't begin until much later, which still didn't include animals rescued by the disaster response team.

It is estimated that from mid 2014 through mid 2018 TMAR rescued four thousand animals. Ninety-nine percent of those animals were dogs and puppies, some were cats and kittens. Plus one fawn. And maybe a raccoon. Or two. And perhaps a goose. But forget you read that. For sure, there was a flock of chickens, one herd of alpacas, some hungry cows and a dozen or so starving horses and well...that's what happens when you rescue animals. You can't pick and choose, you just save them all.

BONUS CHAPTER

Turtle Mountain, meet Florence

Handsome Rob's Story

Just as I was wrapping up some final edits for this book, another hurricane season was underway. Hurricane Florence, the sixth named storm of 2018, was about to make landfall somewhere near the Carolinas.

When the first wave of news hit and confirmed that hurricane Florence was a category 4 storm devastating parts of North Carolina, I made a suggestion that Keith needed a vacation, an animal rescue vacation. The whole team unanimously agreed. We mobilized quickly, volunteers on the ground took over the garage operations, volunteers behind the scenes would keep moving animals along the rescue chain and everyone would pitch in and help Keith from afar. Keith loaded his supplies from last season, strapped the canoe on top of his truck and headed across the country once again to help where help was needed the most.

Over the next week Keith joined up with John NeeSmith again, who drove from Texas to North Carolina to assist with animal rescue efforts and Marshall Furr (real name, I'm seriously jealous), who also drove from Texas. Together the three determined rescuers were able to save all sorts of animals that otherwise could have died, standing stranded in chest high water for days or weeks. Their week was filled with cattle, horses, dogs, cats, alpacas, goats and . . . chickens. But there was one very special rescue that was about to be seen around the world millions of times.

A black and white pit bull, scared and looking very sick, was stranded on top of an almost completely submerged car with no dry ground in sight. Keith waded through the water to check on the scared dog and assess the situation, then went back to him with a kennel and a paddleboard. Keith and John coaxed the scared dog into the kennel then towed him out of the flood waters, paddleboard style.

The dog became known as Handsome Rob.

Handsome Rob was taken to a temporary staging area for displaced dogs. He was seen and treated by a vet as soon as he came through the door. He was in very, very rough shape. Much of which was not because of the water or natural disaster. Handsome Rob had heartworm, lyme disease, ehrlichiosis (canine hemorrhagic fever) broken teeth, lacerations, puncture wounds, bite marks all over his head, neck and ears, in addition to the demeanor a dog displays after being through an extreme amount of trauma.

Keith's week in North Carolina came to a close, he would have to head back but Handsome Rob was still on his mind.

So what do you do when you're the Dog Rescue Guy and live by the motto "when we save a dog, we save him 100 percent?" You drive two thousand miles back to North Carolina and bring him home. That's what you do.

Handsome Rob now lives in North Dakota with Keith at the rescue. His rehabilitation is ongoing. Despite everything he has been through, Rob does not have a single ounce of aggression toward humans or other dogs. Handsome Rob is why rescue matters.

Sometimes grit and heart mixed with a little bit of crazy is what it takes to get the job done when policies and laws fail to protect the most vulnerable among us. Rob's rescue and every one before him, proves that all it takes is one guy in a garage with a team of motivated people behind him to change the world for thousands of dogs and tens of thousands more to come.

Here is a link to watch Handsome Rob's rescue video. http://bit.ly/HandsomeRob

AUTHOR'S NOTE

My mission for writing this book is to raise awareness and funds that alleviate suffering while we work on a long-term solution. By telling the world about the plight of these invisible dogs I've come to love and cry for, I feel good about any small part I've played in helping save them. I write our stories and hope to show that we are genuine, not corrupt or greedy, and to show that the struggles and triumphs of rescue are grueling, rewarding but worth it.

I've learned a lot about the complexity of the issues presented here. Most of which are beyond the scope of anything I am qualified nor want to write about. But here is what I do know. I know that we must be careful with casting blame. That we are not doing our best to take care of each other and the animal kingdom if we are pointing fingers and calling names. These are not problems of the state, county, city, reservation or providence. These are problems for all of humanity to own up to and pitch in to solve.

We must step away from our daily lives and consider the suffering in the 5th Ward, speak with our friends on the First Nations and visit the most vulnerable among us. If we are to help the forgotten dogs we must also help the forgotten people. I don't see tribes, colors, cultures, outsiders, insiders, purples, yellows or greens. I see humans and animals suffering every day and feel a responsibility to get involved. I don't dwell on whose problem it is to fix it or who caused it, or that they are not my problem because I don't live there. I don't live by the notion that this is a reservation issue, nor do I place blame on the politicians or the state, or the tribe or anyone else.

When I ask myself *whose fault is it that so many animals are suffering and so many people have no good options to help them?* I can only come up with one answer that is the cause as much as it is the only solution.

You and me.

Yours and mine.

Us.

We.

Humankind.

IN MEMORY OF COLT ALLERY

A hero remembered never dies.
-Unknown

IN MEMORY OF
ERIC HALVORSON & ROWDY

We can judge the heart of a man by his treatment of animals.
-Immanuel Kant

IN MEMORY OF
SAVANNA LAFONTAINE-GREYWIND

You will never be forgotten.

Some things can never be forgiven.

IN MEMORY OF BUBBA

And Lambchop, John Doe, Big Chief and all the other dogs
that came and went too quickly.

You will be remembered here forever.

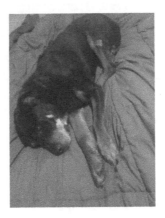

If love could have saved you,
you would have lived forever.
-Unknown

Indian legend says that when a human dies there is a bridge they must cross to enter into Heaven. At the head of the bridge waits every animal that human encountered during their lifetime. The animals, based on what they know of this person, decide which humans may cross the bridge . . . and who is turned away.

The best thing you can do to support an author is to leave an honest review. If you enjoyed Rescue Matters please consider leaving a brief review on Amazon or Goodreads.

If you would like to be notified of upcoming book releases or sales, please visit www.cjenglishauthor.com to sign-up. Thank you for your support! - C.J.

Consider visiting Turtle Mountain Animal Rescue on Facebook or check out www.turtlemountainanimalrescue.org for adoptable dogs, upcoming events or consider making a donation.

ACKNOWLEDGMENTS

To all of the independent rescuers and foster families who are not known or recognized for the lives they save, thank you for taking it upon yourself to make this world a better place for the people and animals. You represent hope and a kinder future.

Thank you to my husband for being my person—the support I need so that I can write and chase tigers. And to Justine for being my study mate three days a week. To Mandee Mckinnon for donating the beautiful book cover, Nicole Hartney for your editing expertise, Erica Rapp for making sure it's polished. Thanks to Stacey Piechowski for your critical eye and Killer Chris Benson for your time helping me with this project. Thank you to Martha Sweeney for your formatting services. To Brenda Olson-Wray for introducing me into the world of dog rescue, you were the gateway my heart was searching for. Thanks to Boz in Australia and Tracy in Canada. To Shelly and Madeline for taking the time to talk and share your stories with me.

From Keith and all of us at TMAR, thank you to Half Brothers Brewery in Grand Forks, ND and Prairie Brothers Brewery in Fargo, ND, Rejuv Medical Aesthetic Clinic, Bell Bank, Bergstrom Cars of Devils Lake, ND, comprised of Lake Chevrolet, Buick GMC, Marketplace Ford Lincoln, and Lake Toyota and Treat Play Love. Cheryl Flesher with Clara Cares. To the Rugby Veterinary clinic that has helped us so many times at so many hours of the day, THANK YOU, Casselton Veterinary service and Dr. Barthalomay, Thank you to Dr. Lori Gossard for everything since the beginning, and to the Lee Veterinary Clinic. Shout out to John NeeSmith and Marshall Furr the Dog father for all your disaster rescue efforts. Jimmy

Monson, Tom Kersten and family, Ross Solwold and Gina Sandgren. Kim Halvorson for her heavenly donation. Jamie Davis for saving so many lives before TMAR was conceived. Tonya and crew at No Dog Left Behind, MN. To all the past and present volunteers who work behind the scenes without a name or recognition but have helped TMAR continue to grow and save lives, a million thanks.

One thousand miigweches to Andy Laverdure, Loren Henry and Myles Brunelle for helping to show Keith the path, and to Jamie Metcalfe for the dare that it couldn't be done.

THANK YOU Aliah Chappell, Trista Zacharias, Andrea Ley Coombs, Danielle Johnson, Franki Wolhart, Katie Kapocius, Kim Gordon, Kimberly Love Hoppe, Krista Majkrak, Lynn Miller, Angie Wollan, Craig Poitra, Tanja Harris, Jessica Miller-Wollan, Bo Cavanaugh, Tanley Ravnaas, Raven Grandbois, Nicole J Rome, Chelsea Thomas, Shannon Dickelman, Sandra Moreau, Amanda Marie Longie, Annette Murphy- Hatz, Ellery and Chad Lystad, Becky Albert, Dierdre Nyquist, Kate Jahner, Kayla Kessels, Olivia Thompson-Johnson, Michael and Lori Anderson, Gary and Jill Lura. Lauren Kupfer, Trenton, Kristine, Chris and Jayme Isakson, Courtney Tylor Knicrt, Abigail Portsmouth, Heather Nelsen, Rhonda and Tommy Belgarde/Baker, Dewey Morinville, Lonna Olson, Dawn Ransom-Herford, Erin Buzick, Jamie Charette, Jeanene Schultz, Joey Marie Anderson, Julie Erdman and a special thank you to Sasha Junkin, for keeping Keith partially sane in times of insanity. To Scott Jasper and Tony Zimmerman for your hands and boots on the ground when Keith needed it most.

Thank you to all the foster families who take in TMAR dogs at all hours of the day and night. Thank you to everyone who has ever driven one puppy one mile, your time and effort may not go recognized but does not go unappreciated. To all the animal rescue organizations that have taken in TMAR dogs and seem to be always squeezing one more in for us. Detroit Lakes Humane Society, 4luvofDog in Fargo, Adopt-a-Pet, Fargo, Homeward Animal Shelter, Diamond in the Ruff, Range Regional Humane Society in Hibbing, MN, Rescue Pets Are Wonderful, Blaine, MN, Lucky Paws Midwest, River Falls, WI, Humane Society of Ottertail County in Fergus Falls, MN, RPAWS, CoCo's Heart and Seth Thomas, Cory Sparks, Kevin Becker at Shutt'er Down Ranch.

Thank you to all the women and men who do the work in the trenches, rehabilitating, going door to door and asking if families need help, those are the unsung heroes in the shadow world of animal rescue.

Thank you Keith Benning for being an inspiration to us all.

Photo Credits: 1. Keith Benning (KB)Gypsy, KB 2. KB, 3. Jennie Belanus (JB) 4. Adobe Stock. Bear KB. 5. KB. Bubba, KB. 6. KB. 7. Aliah Chappell. Smokey, Belcourt Fire Department 8. Trista. Lucas, KB. 9. KB. John Doe, Adobe Stock. 10.CJ English. Band of brothers, Adobe Stock. 11.KB. Fozzy, Adobe Stock. 12.JB. 13. KB. 14.KB. Pickle, KB. Georgie, Lindsay Hall Anderson.15. JB. Arya, KB. 16. KB. 17. Adobe Stock. Daisy, KB. 18. Adobe Stock. Remington, Kayla Kessels. 19. KB. 20. KB. Lenny, Olivia Thompson-Johnson. 21. CJ. Brenda, Brenda Olson-Wray. 22.KB. 23. Kim Halvorson. Bella, KB. 24.KB. Bubba, KB. 25.KB. Big Chief, Adobe Stock. 26. KB. Hudson, JB. 27. CJ. Hope, KB. 28. Anonymous rendering. Glory, Amber Engebretson. Handsome Rob, Gary Lura. Colt Allery, KB. Eric & Rowdy, Kim Halvorson. Savanna, anonymous.

We will right our wrongs and remind humankind of our responsibility to care for you as you have cared for us in our darkest hours. – C.J. English

Made in USA - Kendallville, IN
54299_9780986304248